ALOGOPOIESIS

Amelia Walker

ALOGOPOIESIS

Kite

for Taslima Nasrin (written in Kolkata in 2008)

Graceful as a knife, yet the opposite of violence,
a small kite is trapped in the tree outside my window,
arcing, diving through the morning air.
A ragged wren: black gone grey, sporting its tangles
and tears not as marks of shame, rather trophies
of how far it has flown, and through what storms,
this ordinary kite, this extraordinary kite.

Was it once some child's toy, flown in parks
on sunny weekends, string held taught, no thought of grey?
Perhaps. But at some point, circumstances cut
or forced this kite to cut its own string, to jettison the green
of comforts and soar beyond *beyond*, becoming a sculptor,
carving wild forms in the air.

Such a small kite, such infinite sky, yet it danced
a dance none had dared dream possible,
romancing cyclones, turning tempests into art.
Now it is caught again, snagged by branches,
yet with what small string it has it keeps on dancing,
keeps on daring. Even in breezeless moments, it jiggles
its head as if to say *No*, as if to laugh.

It will not stay trapped long, will not wither like the leaves.
Any moment, this kite will corkscrew *Up! Up! Up!*
will dance more wildly than ever before
this ordinary kite, this extraordinary kite,
the opposite of violence, shining like a knife.

ONE: MEANWHILE IN SUBURBIA

Naming the Tortoise, part one

The child stirs in bed, bladder full, burning. It is dark, and she is scared. She is scared not of the dark, but of what light might reveal. The covers are over her head, with just a small space where her nose pokes through. She wriggles her toes, presses one against the hot water bottle. Still too hot. Yet the sheets remain cold, starchy. They're warmer than the floor, though. She tries rolling on one side. No good. The other. Worse. Shifting to her back, she draws and holds her breath, listens to the white walls groaning, worrying with the things that shift within, like contents of an uneasy bowel.

The clock says two.

Island, part one, version six

silent,
forests grow
and die—

things do not stop happening just because—

sometimes
storms
come—

stubborn
hungry, half-naked,
the surf,
caves,
mountains,
fire-pools—

there is treasure everywhere,
cast away—

no name,
unmapped,
ever shifting—

sand,
lush fruits,
underground springs,
birdsong, uninhibited—

Sensing / Making, version one

The mouth told her, *make more sense.*

She wanted to please. She tried.

Unsure what sense meant, or how to manufacture such a thing, she sought the dictionary. It offered terms, but no recipe. There was sense in senses of judgement: wisdom, fact, practicality. Then there was the sensuous, and sensing. Sound. Taste. Touch. Smell. Sight. Fright. Lust. Love. Motion. Emotion. A sense of fun. Humour. Occasion. Direction. South. East. Sky. Sea. Waves, tides, and their rises. Moons and stars. Rhythms and dancing. Sense as experience, common and uncommon. Knowledge. Intuition. To know without knowing how one knows. A shared sense—connection.

These senses, to her, all seemed like moments snatched from longer dreams recurring differently in the minds of countless sleepers. She decided to piece them together, to make something from them—make something she hoped might make sense enough to please the mouth.

And so she turned words into cards. With the cards she built houses. Then towers, halls, stations, malls, cemeteries. A small world. Fragile. Detailed. Like the real one.

She took her world to the mouth. Stood. Waited. Trembling.

The mouth opened wide. In its throat was an eye. The mouth drew breath. Deep. Then blew her world down.

Try again, the mouth said.

So she tried.

This time she went straight to the source. To sense. Pressing her ears to beehives, she gathered their buzz, stewed it in her tear ducts, then cried mead for the mouth to drink.

The mouth spat. Grimaced. *Try again.*

She undressed herself for the ocean, let it sing through her insides. And out. From sheets of foam, she made a giant bed, soft and waiting.

The mouth would not lie down.

She grew wings just to feel them clipped, busted limbs for the sake of healing. From ground feathers and bones, she made sculptures of tiny hearts—really moving, really beating.

The mouth barely looked, refused to touch.

After that, she rode her bicycle across snow-covered beaches, slept inside mountains of sun. She ate to know tastes and starved to taste more. She sat in sound, danced with quiet. Time came and danced too, gifted her a sense of loss, and thus gratitude for everything still left to lose.

She tried sharing her gifts with the mouth. It remained closed, turned away, until finally she stopped and asked:

What is sense? How can I make it?

The mouth opened—wide, then wider. From it rushed a freezing tide of silence.

The Perfect Front Lawn, version two

Lawn mattered in 1980s Australia

—bees—clover—getting stung—

Calamine skin-upon-skin:
ritual, penance, salve.

Defeated playing games
good girls must outgrow

—wall—window—inside—

freckles paling, skirt ironed
in place

watching father with his Victa mower

—up—back—up—back—

straight, uniform
engine vibrations through the floor.

Afterwards: cut blades and two-stroke.

How would it feel—to start a mower with just one pull?

THE WOMAN WITH THE DISOBEDIENT HEAD, PART ONE

MaggieMem has come unglued. in the middle of a peak-hour train carriage. what a pain.

The Man next to MaggieMem emits a sharp aroma. his large, warm body is pressed close to MaggieMem's, as are the bodies of several other strangers. anonymous knees and elbows jutting, poking, jiggling and jabbing whenever the train slows into a station or speeds up again. every now and then somebody—quite often MaggieMem—murmurs an apology. but there are only so many times the word 'sorry' can sound sincere. particularly at this hour of the morning.

Through the Cracks, version three

dishes
dishes

filthy, out of order

make them clean,
put them where they belong

hot water,
detergent—sometimes lavender, sometimes lemon—

plates plain white,
K Mart's standard issue
—easy to source replacements

wine glasses,
vegemite jars

right parts in their rightful order:

glassware before crockery

THE BLACK SHOES, VERSION TWO

purchased for work,
worn with thick stockings, a pencil skirt.

take but the tiniest of steps,
always in straight, straight lines—

a kind of dancing,
moving to a beat—click clack, like castanets—fast—

not a waltz, nor a tango, oh no,
more like a march, a military two-step,

torso rigid, frenetic legs, patterns drilled in
—keep up—
the thought
clicking, like a second hand—
Bitch, you're paid to dance

blisters,
aches in legs
—at night,
still dancing, taking orders

can't say why, just how it is, how it seems it's always been—

click clack
like wagging tongues,
like laughter.

Collingwood Daze, version two

and then, spinning, pupils wide

mouths of those sideshow clowns moving fast *toofast*

—a party—

such a good party
—the best

—whichever it was—

walls at weird angles,
breathing water,

swimming,
drowning

—cool *oh so* cool—

The Girls, The Guys,
undiscovered Kerouacs, fun to be around,

saying THIS

is IT

and and and and and and and and and and and and and and
and and
and and and and and and and and and

Hungry, part one

Atop a plateau surrounded by sheer cliff face, surrounded by desert, surrounded by volcanoes sits a box, not unlike the admission boxes outside rides at a fairground. On the front of this box is a square white placard, painted with black squiggles indecipherable to all except those within the organisation they denote The Department of New Beginnings.

Inside the box is The Official. The age, race, gender, style of dress, psycho-spiritual persuasion and ice-cream flavour preferences of The Official are irrelevant, except to say that they do not differ significantly from the age, race, gender, style of dress, psycho-spiritual persuasion, and ice-cream flavour preferences of all the others who sit in this box on various days, covering various shifts. It is important to say *The* Official as opposed to *an* or *that*. 'An official' might suffice on days off, at cocktail parties, when someone asks, 'So what do you do?' But during opening hours, it's The Official. Regardless how many shift changes might occur in the serving of one applicant, every official is The Official and ought to be treated as such.

Chronics, version two

oven clock error:
four zeroes
flashing
midnight
blue Ohs
like square mouths, screaming—

on the floor

—how long? clock
still broken
somebody laughing
why?

help

white corridors, everything retro space age. sucked along. breathless vortex. exposed. pine-o-clean and salt damp.

shaking, shrunken.
then. then. then—

years later, it's still midnight.

Taking Time, part one, version six

weeks,
days

nothing.

No
no
no,
not even

farewell

Meanwhile in Suburbia / Auto-cento one

white walls groaning, worrying
(things do not stop happening just because)

South. East. Sky. Sea. Waves, tides,
and their rises. Moons and stars. Rhythms
and dancing
                                        up—back—up—back—

anonymous knees and elbows
jutting, poking, jiggling and jabbing

filthy, out of order

take but the tiniest of steps,
always in straight, straight lines

swimming
            drowning

cool oh so cool

on days off, at cocktail parties,
sucked along. breathless vortex. exposed.

Then. Then. Then.

No
no
no

TWO: BEAUTIFUL PEOPLE

for Nobody, in Particular, part one

There was a girl who dressed in woodsmoke
and spoke in shades of Autumn.
Her words swirled, leafy will o wisps. Her eyes
were colours of laughing. She danced

in shadows, played tricks on the light.
She held all seasons, buried in her skin.
At the right touch, Spring would rush
to the surface: a field of scarlet daffodils.

Naming the Tortoise, part two

The child wriggles violently now. Her abdomen feels on fire. Maybe she could piss the bed. It would be warm. For a while. She'd get in trouble. But so what? Trouble happens anyway. Constantly. The real problem would be lying in the piss once it went cold. And burning. She takes a breath. Counts to ten. One, two … On nine, she falters. Start again … seven, eight … This time, on ten, she throws back the covers and swings her legs out. Feet on floor. Icy! No choice. She springs, one patch of carpet to the next.

Then, she freezes—no longer cold, just frozen.

A Story not about Green

Green is not the main character in this drama. Green would like to be, but casting was in the hands of other directors. Besides, the whole plot was mapped out years ago, woven from stories told and re-told, the same stories that tell us and through which we tell who and what and how to be. Oh no, Green did not need telling. Green knew, had known from the start, the main characters would be red and blue and yellow—those loud suck-holes of attention. And Green, Green was resolved to be a scene-filler, a walk-in-walk-out line at various odd and scattered moments—comic relief, a chance for the audience to breathe out, breathe in, prepare for the next actually relevant twist. Green was, yes, a leaf, a frail leaf clinging shakily to the long branch of a fading tree, secondary even to brown.

Island, part one, version five

Sailors wreck themselves.
Do not invite them.
Do not ask that they leave.

Remain silent, as always, never still.

Forests grow and die.
Beasts breed and battle

Things do not stop happening
just because nobody sees or records.

Still, they come—stubborn Selkirks
and yearning Crusoes—hungry, half-naked,
half-clothed in the surf that swept them ashore.

They come for adventure, decrying dullness
—their homelands, their mothers,
those safe and sensible lives
they then rebuild
frantically

—frightened of caves, forests, mountains, fire-pools.

There is treasure everywhere,
but they don't know how to look.

At the first opportunity,
s.o.s. and race away.

Sensing / Making, version two

She wanted to please. She tried.
Unsure, she sought Knowledge.
She turned words into houses, stations, malls, cemeteries.
A small world.

She stood, trembling, drew breath. Deep.

Try again.

She tried pressing her ears to beehives,
gathered their buzz, then cried mead.

Try again.

She undressed and grew wings
—tiny hearts, moving, beating.

She rode across snow-covered beaches,
slept inside mountains of sun,
ate to know tastes and starved to taste more,
sat in sound, danced with quiet,
gifted her everything until finally she stopped

and then rushed freezing silence.

Woman Buying Fish

Response to the painting 'Fischmarkt' by Carl Moser

So this is wifehood,
she thinks, staring down
at sprawled, once-living creatures,
their goop eyes
staring up.

She must choose
from this array of flesh
still wet with ocean currents, surging
with blood, becalmed,
starting to stink

—choose one,
take it home, remove head,
tail, bone, scales
so nobody will know
this thing once had eyes
like mirrors, eyes that held
dreams beyond
the seen, eyes

and a body that pulsed,
danced unfrightened
before that moment it was caught,
stunned, sliced, cleaned, and steamed,
splayed out soft and pink
on a white plate,
ready, waiting
to be swallowed.

LargeMan is soft, slightly moist. like a supermarket brie left out in the sun. his face more jahrlsberg. pale and shiny with yawning black pores. MaggieMem imagines that if she were to blow across his face—softly, ever so softly—he might whistle. like an empty beer bottle or some curious moon-shaped flute. his smell is cheesish too, though now we are definitely moving towards the aged varieties. a crumbly cheddar or fruity blue vein. and garlic. definite undertones of garlic. perhaps, after all, beneath the protective white shirt paunch he is not a man but a generous party platter, stacked high with mettwurst, gherkins, gleaming baby octopus—and of course—cheese.

MaggieMem is thankful for the man's smell. it completely hides the glue. she places a hand beneath her chin, feigning nonchalance, revealing (she hopes) nothing of the intense concentration it takes to maintain her balancing act. the hand's actual purpose is to keep her head in place.

Hungry, part two

The opening hours of The Department seem to many people random and inexplicable. In fact, they are quite straightforwardly laid out in a timetable that can be obtained from The Department itself. Of course, any application for a timetable must be dealt with during opening hours, and must gain The Official's approval.

A woman clambers onto the plateau. From all fours, she rises unsteadily upon feet bare and shredded from her climb. She is panting, so dehydrated she has ceased to sweat. Her age, race, gender, style of dress, religion and ice-cream flavour preferences differ markedly from those of The Official. She has mud on her face and an odour of long journeying. The Official cringes as she approaches the box. Why do these people never bother to put any time into their presentation?

Taking Time, part one, version five

three weeks and four days since
touched
in any way.

nothing. no hugs, no handshakes, no high fives. not even—

breathing,
wishing
but understanding

these things take time.

the farewell kiss,
the chill air,
hunger,
heat,
lips,
skin.

busy.
busy.
busy.

Sundori

a composite character woven from recollections of my time in Kolkata

Her name was Sundori.
No, it wasn't. It was Pushpa.
Sundori was what I called her
as I cleaned her wounds and settled her
in her bed at the volunteer-run shelter.
Sundori Pushpa: *Beautiful Pushpa, Beautiful Flower.*

She'd been burned.
Her husband had burned her
because she'd been beautiful—and still was,
fine cheekbones pressing through rippled skin
that had, like wax, melted then frozen,
the trauma moment fixed forever.

Everyone could see it. Even those Americans
who stayed just one day and donated thousands
for surgery to sculpt new lids round her blinded eyes.
But she refused. And when pushed, broke forth,
running for the junk heap, screaming *Na! Na! Naaaa!*
as she rubbed existing wounds in filth.

Sundori Pushpa, I cooed later,
fishing with tweezers for deep-lodged debris.
Na, she said again, this time in a whisper
before tears filled her eyes.
Later, they filled mine, too, when I realised:
of all thinkable words, all names,
I'd picked the worst, the most violent.

Beautiful People / Auto-cento two

a field of scarlet daffodils
—warm. for a while

—breathe out, breathe in, prepare—

silent, as always, never still—

Try again.
tried.
Try again.
undressed.

So this is wifehood.

a supermarket brie
left out in the sun.
empty beer bottle,
moon-shaped flute

—she has ceased to sweat—

breathing,
wishing
but understanding

—rippled skin
like wax, melted then frozen—

a simple solution

in this moment—the next—the next—

Through the Cracks, version two

washed a lot of dishes at Clauscen Street. not because anybody said, or even to try and be nice. washing dishes is an ABC equation: take things that are filthy, strewn out of order, make them clean—somehow new again—put them in places where they belong. hot water is a nice thing in winter. chilblains worth it. waking at two, three, four a.m., trace fingers of one hand over bumpy knuckles of the other, know one thing—

detergent—sometimes lavender, sometimes lemon. plates mostly of seventies vintage—big flowers and geometric arrays of shapes in faded shades of what would once have been lime green, orange and/or brown—acquired at op shops and garage sales and/or left behind by previous housemates. all similar, none precisely the same—dishes—

a simple solution to the ever-pressing question of this moment—and the next—and the next—

flowers too faded, too many pieces missing, cracked. replaced with plain white—standard issue, easy to source. wept. wept for those gone, long as memory, into brokenness—

keep breathing. lavender-scented dishwater. the window. things never said out loud. didn't like. stupid. mouth shut. glassware before crockery.

THREE: LANGUAGE LESSONS

Waking up to White, version one

I have forgotten when it was. I have forgotten who. My mother or my father, most likely. At some point one of them sat me down and fed me this syllable.

White.

White is a colour. White is not a colour. A not-colour. White is black, but opposite. White is absence of colour … unless we're talking light, then white is what happens when all the other colours climb into bed together.

White light. White light. Go towards it. Don't go towards it. At sixteen I lay down and listened to Lou Reed for days. I have a tattoo of Lady MacBeth, only my lovers can see.

White dresses for weddings. White flags for surrender. Omo will make your whites whiter, your colours brighter. In some cultures white means death.

White Christmas in White Australia is Forty Six Celsius White. White trash. White washed. Washing down the white water storm pipes out out into the great white wash. The water is rising. White houses will be swallowed. Or eaten by white ants. Who remembers white sand? Snow. Sometimes they say that when they mean something else.

White bread. Sticks to the roof of your mouth. White bread. Sticks inside your bowel. White bread body, wash it down with red wine. Careful. You can't get blood stains out of white.
She ate an apple and slept for a long time. White light. White light. White light.

Her inner arms were pale and puckered with miniature kiss shadows white. None woke her. The ambulance white. The emergency department walls white. My ironed starchy nurse's shirt white. The big bag and its plastic zipper white. The barely creased sheets. I stripped them away, breathed the smell of detergent, the smell of white.

Washed my hands and the sink drained

white.

Hungry, part three

'Hungry!' the woman exclaims, leaning so close to the box window that The Official can smell the acid of her empty stomach propelled on her breath.

The Official coughs, shuffles some papers, shifts left then right atop the cracked vinyl chair, glances at the clock and coughs again.

'Your name?'

'Hungry. I am Hungry,' the woman repeats.

The Official checks the time.

'That is unfortunate, but irrelevant to the matter at hand. I can do nothing for your application if you cannot first tell me your name.'

'Hungry,' the woman says yet again, now adding hand gestures, pointing frantically to herself.

The Official sighs.

Now the woman attempts to make other sounds. She makes them in The Official's language, but The Official still doesn't comprehend. The problem is her mouth. Just as lapping ocean waves will over millions of years wear grooves and hollows in solid rock, the curves of this woman's palette, forged over a lifetime, are fine-tuned for songs there is no point singing here.

'My name is Hungry,' she finally manages.

Naming the Tortoise, part three

It's there again, like she feared it would be. A strange shape in the centre of the hallway, long-necked with sad black eyes. It's just a dream, the child tells herself. One of those dreams that happens when you're not in bed or sleeping. But you're dreaming nonetheless, because what's happening isn't happening—what isn't, is.

It's just a dream, the child tells herself. And she believes herself. It's a dream she's had and woken from countless times before. Still. There's nothing just about dreams when they're coming straight towards you.

Language Lesson

Lesbian.
My first exposure
to this word
was being called one
in year two.

A phlegmy spit ball,
it hit me square
between the eyes.
Nothing I did,
nothing I said
could wipe it away.

First strike
and target susceptibility confirmed,
I was socked by endless rounds
from all directions
as the whole school took aim
and fired.

What did it mean?
The school dictionary leapt straight
from *leprosy* to *less*:
Was lesbian the unspeakable seam,
the abyss those two things shared?

This theory matched the tone
of my teacher's voice
when I asked, *What's a lesbian?*
and she replied,
That's a bad word—never say it.

Relief came, for me at least,
the morning I arrived to a circle
of peers gathered, crow-like,
round one of the smaller boys
cawing *Poof, Poof, Poof.*

What did it mean?
I didn't care.
The attention was off me.
I was invited to join in
and so I did,
breathing relief
to be back in the fold.

Poof, Poof, Poof.

This time, I didn't bother
with dictionaries or my teacher.
I knew as much as I needed:

whatever *Poof,*
whatever *Lesbian* meant,
I did not want to be one.

I washed a lot of dishes at Clauscen Street. Not because anybody said I should or even to try and be nice. It was just what I felt like doing. Washing dishes is an ABC equation: take things that are filthy, all strewn out of order, and make them clean—somehow new again—then put them in places where they belong. Hot water is a nice thing in the Melbourne winter, too. I got chilblains, but they were worth it. Waking at two, three, four a.m., I'd trace the fingers of one hand over the bumpy knuckles of my other and know I wasn't totally adrift: one thing I did in life, at least, was useful and made a difference, if only to the state of our kitchen.

We used Trix detergent—sometimes lavender, sometimes lemon. I preferred the lavender. It's calming, whereas the lemon could put me on edge. Our plates were mostly of seventies vintage—big flowers and geometric arrays of shapes in faded shades of what would once have been lime green, orange and/or brown—acquired at op shops and garage sales and/or left behind by housemates who had lived there before us. They were all similar, and none precisely the same—the plates, that is. Nearly all of them were chipped. Trav blamed this on Jake, who he reckoned was clumsy. But Trav also blamed Jake for all the beer stains on the carpet, whereas I had witnessed events suggesting otherwise. I just nodded when he said it, though—let him rave and feel justified. It wasn't worth an argument.

Trav was my boyfriend, Jake our other housemate. I hadn't really planned, at twenty-one, to be living with a boyfriend—especially not after just two months. But when my previous sharehouse fell apart unexpectedly, he offered, and I was spending most nights there anyway at that stage, so it seemed a simple solution. Like dishes. Dishes were a simple solution to the ever-pressing question of what I should be doing in this moment—and the next—and the next—

Those plates resembled the set my parents owned when I was small and threw out when I was nine or so: the flowers were too faded, too many pieces were missing or cracked. Mum and Dad replaced our warm, wonderful flower plates with a plain white set—K-Mart's standard issue, which made it easy to source matching replacements whenever the need arose. I wept. I wept for those gone plates, the source of my sustenance for as long as memory stretched. Then at Clauscen Street I got them back. Not the same plates, but close enough, probably given away under similar circumstances—and prior to that, purchased under similar circumstances too. They were, I suppose, not so different from the white plates after all. They were simply the standard issue of a time when the standard was a little more out there: mass produced, sold cheaply to newlyweds wide-eyed over their spanking new laminex and mortgages.

Trav and I were the farthest thing imaginable from those newlyweds, I used to think as I traced my chilblained fingers along the patterns of cracks in the plates. I liked the cracks. They suggested stories I couldn't read, but knew were there, and lent, I thought, an inadvertent kind of wabi sabi quality—an individuality, an artfulness to the otherwise ultimately generic, purpose-driven objects. In truth, I knew almost nothing about wabi sabi except that people whose clothes were cooler than mine had been saying it a lot at recent parties. In truth, it may not have been the cracks themselves I liked, but the act of liking the cracks—liking the very thing that had given others a basis to reject these beautiful objects, to call them ugly. I liked being the one to see through all that, to see the cracks as beauty. Running my fingers along them felt, sometimes, like crawling inside them, into a place that was dark and warm and safe. The brokenness of the plates was a brokenness that spoke of ways to fit.

The other attraction to dishes was that they seemed a thing I couldn't get wrong—or so I thought. Then Trav cut sick at me for washing plates before glassware. For fuck's sake, how stupid are you? You're making the wine glasses cloudy. By wine glasses he meant vegemite jars. Part of me wanted to say that if he wanted it done his way he could do it himself. But I was worried he would, and then what would I do at two, three, four a.m.?

After that I made sure not just to clean up the mess, but to clean the right parts of the mess in their rightful order. Trav didn't complain again. Nor did he acknowledge the improvement. But then, he was passed out a lot of the time. I didn't mind. I was happy just to keep breathing the lavender-scented dishwater that made me feel so warm. Bliss: staring through the window, thinking things I never said out loud because who would I say them to? They were too stupid. For instance, I dreamed sometimes about pasting signs on all the university and bookstore notice boards, inviting fellow share house dwellers to join a great plate swap on our lawn. The idea was that if we pooled enough people with enough mixed-up plate sets, we'd be able to sort all the stray pieces into matching sets. Then everybody could take a set home and our kitchens, our lives would be like new, like it was nineteen seventy-five once more, or maybe even nineteen fifty-three. Except was that what I wanted? I didn't know. All I knew was that I didn't like being called stupid. So, I kept my mouth shut and made certain to wash glassware before crockery.

Island, part one, version four

Sailors wreck themselves upon me.
I do not invite them. I do not ask that they leave.

I remain silent, as always, never still. My forests grow
and die. Beasts breed and battle within me. I spurt lava
from high peaks and hidden aqueducts.

These things do not stop happening just because nobody sees
or records.

Sometimes I am kind, providing nourishment.
Sometimes I lash out with storms and predators.

Still, they come to me,
stubborn Selkirks and yearning Crusoes.
They come hungry, half-naked, half-clothed
in delusions their skill, not the surf, swept them ashore.

And yes, there came one Crusoe who was a woman.

The men came fleeing their mothers,
but she came fleeing the men.

She wasn't frightened of my caves.
Her feet were soft upon my sand.
I wanted her to walk and walk and walk.

Taking Time, part one, version four

three weeks and four days since
last saw you,
last made love.

afterwards
in bed, holding,
warm, breathing,
wishing but understanding

these things take time. then

the farewell kiss,
the chill air,
hunger for heat
lips,
skin,
seeing you again.

what could we do?
busy. busy. busy.

appointments,
deadlines,
to-do lists—

around the edges,
moments to explore
becoming, together.

Sensing / Making, version three

her dictionary offered no Rhythms

common and uncommon knowing
to her seemed snatched dreams
recurring differently

something Fragile took her In
its throat
drew her down.
again

time went to her ears
gathered in her tear ducts for to drink the ocean

her lie grew feathers
bones refused to touch
her mountains of sound
and her everything left

her mouth remained
closed

why this morning, of all mornings? MaggieMem wonders as a hot rivulet of melted glue darts its path along collarbone, down to the catchments of her underwire. damn—a brand new bra. she checklists the events of her morning, trying to pin-point a cause. it is Wednesday. she would hardly be surprised if this occurred on a Monday, but Wednesday carries no extraordinary stress. she woke early and had plenty of time to enjoy her coffee (MaggieMem is sure low caffeine levels reduce the stability of her glue). perhaps it was the kid with the earphones. apishly long-limbed, enough gel in his hair to enbalm an emu, he ambled up to the station and parked his shiny boxer-shorts-hanging-out-of-low-pants arse right next to MaggieMem. for such a scrawny specimen, he managed to fill considerable space with his aura of hot chips and muffly *doofdoofdoof.*

Language lessons / Auto-cento three

She ate an apple and slept for a long time

because
filthy
out of order

again, like she feared

a dream,
a dream she's had and woken from countless times before

What did it mean?

the cracked vinyl chair,
the clock,
sailors, forests, beasts
hungry

for heat,
lips,
skin.

No recipe
for the glue
to keep her head in place—

a weight
—Why don't they just—?

full of words
silent

Women like that

I just don't understand women like that,

this lady in the supermarket is saying,
gesturing to a tabloid tableau
of some young starlet trying, failing to hide
black eye and tears.

Why don't they just get up, get out
and away?

I stand by, full of words …
… silent.

Two years with you taught me silence as an art
I can't unlearn, even now, thirteen years
since that day I threw my life onto a friend's trailer,
hurrying because we weren't sure when you'd be home

—thirteen years since, yes, I got up and got out
because days earlier you'd picked me up and thrown me
across the room. I remember flying

—thwack—

the wall—my head—then black—then red—

then you, crying in my arms
like you were always crying.

See, what the lady in the supermarket can't know
is how much time women like us spend comforting
our fragile monsters, who don't so much cage us
as lure us into their own cages
from which they can't escape.

Your cage was really your father's—aftershocks
of a war for which neither of us were born
and because of which you were always crying,
always saying sorry, and I, I would tell you,
it was okay, I didn't mind
that you'd called me dumb and ugly, after all
you'd never hit me …

Yeah, okay, you'd locked me in the house
and chased me round, but still
you hadn't hit me …
Alright, so sometimes you fucked me in my sleep,
sometimes I thought you'd hit me
if I didn't do what you wanted
But that was just in my head
because I always gave you what you wanted
(and wanted, and wanted …)

No, you never ever hit me. But that day
you picked me up and threw me … that was enough
for me to say, *Enough*. I got up and got out.
Did I get away?

I learned to box, travelled, returned to study,
started dating again—fell
into something I called love, for seven years
without feeling it. But …

he had a job, didn't drink, didn't lose his shit
every night. For sure he'd never hit me
—nor throw me, nor lock me in the house
nor fuck me without consent. But …

There were also other things he never gave me,
things I needed.

Eventually, again, I got up,
got out. Now, after all these years …

… Still silent
while a stranger speaks and speaks
of what she doesn't and can't understand.

This is how I know, despite getting up and out,
I'm yet to get away.

Dra(a)g

I'm fascinated by drag—this word passed mouth
to mouth, down and across frayed lines of shifting time/s
and cultures. Like *love, lust, hate, hope, ache, cry, queer*
and *wonder* it can be both noun and verb, act/ion and
object(ion). For centuries in English, writers and speakers
have *dragged*, have called things *drags*—yet differently:

In the thirteenth and fourteenth centuries, *dragge*
and *draggen* were tied to fishing—dragnets and grappling
hooks or *grapnel*: Swedish, *dragg*, from Old Norse, *dragga*,
meaning load. Today, when we drag, we bear a weight. Yes,
even when we carry it off, it can weigh us, wear us down.
But like fishers, we are searchers, braving beyond shores
and surfaces, sifting slippery treasures from murk into shine.

By the fifteenth century, *drag* had gathered force
—and violence—towards not only *pulling*, but also, *away*
as rule-breakers and demonstrators are at times pulled
and locked away (let's not forget the World War Two pilots
arrested in Georgia for wearing pants after dark).
Yet dragging away—*pulling and (a)parting*—implies counter
pull(s) *back*: resistance … retardation … slowing … down …
as Shakespearean actors in heavy skirts were slowed
—perhaps why we speak of drag kings and queens today.

Or … could drag as performance be cut, somehow
from the same cloth as *dragen*—the Dutch verb
for *to carry* or *wear*? *Ik draag kleren* means I wear clothes
(of any kind). From this comes *gedrag*: behaviour—a way
of acting, though not a formal act. *Wangedragen* is mis-
behaving, acting up, and *verdragen* endurance: surviving.

FOUR: CHILDHOOD / GAMES

Sensing / Making, version four

Told to please, she sought direction.
Waves, tides, and their rises, to her, seemed like houses.
She opened wide, drew breath.

Then blew her world down.

She cried.

Try again.

Wings busted, she refused.
Gifted a sense of loss
and thus gratitude,
her mouth remained closed
until she stopped
and asked:

What is I?

Snakes and Ladders, version one

Snakes and ladders always seemed such a stupid game. There was no control, beyond knowing how to roll the dice so certain numbers came up—and if you did that you were cheating. Otherwise, everything was left to chance, gravity and landing on the right squares while other players hit the wrong ones. Sometimes you could think yourself so close …

Then, three squares before the finish line you'd hit that damn biggest-of-all snakes snake and be sent spiralling down down down back to the very bottom rung. Or, equally, you might have been climbing, slowly, steadily, inching just that little way each time, and then someone who'd been way behind would hit the big ladder and win the whole shebang.

The set we owned had pictures of children on the squares at the tops and bottom of the ladders and snakes. The children all had white skin. It was eighties Australia. At the bottoms of the ladders they were doing things like studying or working hard. Then, at the tops, they were getting degrees, or lots of money.

The children at the tops of the snakes were doing things like stealing, or being lazy, then sliding into consequences. The game taught me it was bad to eat and get fat. I felt shame when I hit a snake—guilty, like I'd really done whatever the picture condemned, when in truth I'd simply followed the rules, rolled the dice and landed on the wrong square.

In retrospect, it taught me a lot about life.
A stupid game, for sure.

Hungry, part four

'Hungry is a state, not a name,' The Official informs the woman.

She tilts her head and furrows her brow, perhaps working to process the sounds he has uttered. Or perhaps she is searching for words to reply that there are many different kinds of names beyond those The Official has encountered, and that in places where The Official hasn't been, names among other sounds and symbols are used in ways wildly exceeding anything of which The Official has dreamed.

But if this is what she is thinking, she hasn't the words to convey it. Not in The Official's language, at least.

'Hungry is my name, true,' is all she says.

Naming the Tortoise, part four

It's a lumbering sage of a creature, knee high, shell so wide it clinks the corridor walls as the four legs creeps their inevitable way forth. The child holds her breath, wonders whether it can move faster, if it wants to. Does it have teeth? Would it bite?

The neck wrinkles and stretches, folds of leather rippling as the head turns to peer one way, then the other. Set deep in the face are eyes like burnt out stars. Yes, the creature has a face. The creature is a tortoise, and the tortoise has a name. It's a name the child has never heard spoken. Who would or could speak the name of that which doesn't exist? Logically, it should have no name of which to speak. Yet the child hears it in her head. An echo with no source. Unlike most echoes, it grows louder, not softer. It grows and spreads, enters the child's throat. It chokes. It burns. The child wants it out. Wants to scream. Or at least whisper.

She opens her mouth. Draws a breath. Swallows hard. Straightens her spine. Stays in silence.

Taking Time, part one, version three

It's three weeks and four days since I touched you,
since we last made love.

Afterwards, we lay in my bed
holding one another: warm, breathing,
me wishing you could stay
but understanding when you said,
Yes, but these things take time.

Then the farewell kiss by your car,
the chill air priming my hunger
for heat,
lips,
skin,
seeing you again.

I thought it would be a week.

But you were busy. I was busy.
We were two busy women, striving—

around the edges
moments to meet and explore
becoming, together.

Two Truths, One Lie

I've visited America only three times, briefly,
but I may as well have lived there all my life.
After we split, my first boyfriend became a nazi
and later, a real estate agent.
I've never jumped out of a plane.

My favourite colour is green, not pink.
A man I knew from childhood died in a house fire,
days after the psych ward discharged him,
saying he wasn't really that depressed.
I've jumped from many planes.

The first girl I kissed told me the next day,
she did it in public to impress a guy she liked.
My first job was cash in hand, but I got more
if I took cash in back pocket.
I've never jumped out of a plane.

This one time after youth group, a Catholic priest,
driving me home, confessed he was drunk.
My first taste of pot was at Suzuki school
and I wasn't sure if I liked it.
I've jumped from lots of planes.

As a child I thought war was a TV show
the grown-ups were too mean to let me watch.
The second time I tried pot was the last:
for real, I just don't like it.
Never have I jumped from a plane.

When I tried heroin, I felt woozy,
then bored, and never took it again.
I've lived in America all my life
despite visiting only three times.
Yes, I've jumped from planes.

This one time, a Catholic priest
who was driving me home
confessed that he was drunk.
My favourite colour is green, not pink.
Never ever have I jumped from a plane.

After my first boyfriend and I split,
he became a nazi, then a real estate agent.
The first girl I kissed told me the next day
she only did it to impress some guy.
From countless planes, yes, I have jumped.

My first taste of pot was at Suzuki school
and my second was my last: I just don't like it.
When I tried heroin, it made me woozy,
then bored.
No, I've never jumped from a plane.

When I was a child, I snuck behind the couch
to watch TV shows my parents banned, like war.
My first job was cash in hand,
and I cashed in bonuses aplenty.
For real. I have jumped from planes.

But seriously. My favourite colour is pink,
not green. And I'm still sad for that man I knew
in childhood, the one who died in a fire
because he wasn't really that depressed.
This one time, I jumped from a plane.

THE GAME OF BARBIES, VERSION ONE

In nineteen-eighty seven, my mother's take on feminism was buying me Doctor Barbie. I loved Barbie. They all said. The adults. I was a girly girl—they said—and I was. Because I played—and played and played and played and played with those Barbies and at birthdays even asked for more Barbies. Presumably I asked for Barbies because I liked Barbies.

Or did I just like the game of Barbies? Because I was good at it. It was what I knew. I'd had training and knew how to play, knew how to win. So I thought. Yes, there is winning with barbies. The rules might not be written down, the scores never lit up or announced. But points are tallied and prizes awarded all the same. Likewise, fouls are called, offenders disqualified. It seems unfair, since boundaries and goalposts alike are never more than guessed at. And they shift. But that's the point. What makes winning at Barbies so special and so hard is that the game itself is so much more, so much less than what seems to be at play.

As a child, I got good at Barbies. So I thought. But it wasn't just me playing. It wasn't just my game. Getting good is not the same as winning. All the while, I was being played, even as I fancied myself playing at much, much more. The Barbies, after all, were tokens, and I played with them because they were in my hands, a fee I willingly paid to enter the adults' game.

Island, part one, version three

I am not a man. not a woman.
Countries are referred to with the pronoun *she*,
but I am no country.

My name is I. I am land. I shift
break off, float, resurface. Sometimes tropical,
sometimes cold. I am no particular island.
I am *the* island, the only one
of many.

And yes, one Crusoe was a woman.

She wasn't frightened of my caves. Darkness
was the very thing she sought.
Her feet were soft upon my sand.
I wanted her to walk and walk and walk.

I did what I don't often do: I made myself lush
for her, provided all she could want, and more.

My tree-arms ached with the weight of ripe fruits.
She preferred meat. She had a gun.
Still, her feet on my sand remained worth giving.

Safety, warmth, shelter, food, birdsong, beauty. Life.

I let her build huts
topple trees and plough fields
loathe to so much as sweep her footprints from my shore.

Childhood / Games / Auto-cento four

Make, make, make sense
please

—no control,
a stupid game—

unfortunate, but irrelevant.
The problem is her mouth.

It chokes. It burns.

Pink,
not green.

Three weeks and four days since—

a sudden AH,
red and bloody

pulsing
thrashing
wondering

The only one of many.
All similar, none precisely the same.

Why this morning, of all mornings?

The game itself is so much more,
so much less than what seems to be at play.

Through the Cracks, version four

When I was small, nine or so,
the flowers were too faded,
too many pieces missing or cracked.

Mum and Dad replaced our warm, wonderful plates
with a plain white set—K-Mart's standard issue,
easy to source replacements whenever need arose.

I wept. I wept for those gone plates.

Then at Clauscen Street I got them back.
Not the same plates, but close enough,
probably given away under similar circumstances
—and purchased, too.

They were not so different from the white plates after all:
mass produced, sold cheaply to newlyweds
wide-eyed over spanking new laminex
and mortgages.

Trav and I were the farthest thing
from those newlyweds, I used to think,
staring through the window,
stupid mouth shut.

THE WOMAN WITH THE DISOBEDIENT HEAD, PART FOUR

MaggieMem has always felt nervous around electronic devices, and electronic music is definite cause for concern. particularly when it repeats itself. yeah yeah ooh baby particularly when it repeats itself ooh yeah baby doll. not to mention the frequencies. MaggieMem is not A Scientist. she keeps a salt crystal by her bed. she doesn't know the reason but she knows about the buzzy hummy shivering that technology creates—something to do with isotopes jiggling and clashing against one another, nano-scale mosh pits. MaggieMem would never voice these notions, of course. particularly not to her Brother who really is A Scientist, has letters after his name that prove it and is far too clever to ever even momentarily think about thinking such things. MaggieMem thinks things. such things! she used to try not thinking, but the second she stopped thinking about not thinking the same old thoughts broke through—even more numerous, more ridiculous after extra time to breed and mutate. these days MaggieMem just thinks and keeps her mouth shut.

<<*next stop city central*>>
<<*next stop city central*>>

Owned

I heart you, the girl says
with her mouth, for the first time,
though her fingers have endlessly pressed
this message via keys
and codes, symbols and screens.

She's an expert
when it comes to buttons.
But her tongue is unprepared
for the shape of what she's saying. The sound
brings out a sudden AH, slices the skin
of her sentence, revealing
at the centre, not some goofy kitten
in pixels and pink, but an organ,
red and bloody.

I heart you too, the boy doesn't say
with his mouth. He utters not one word
and yet his hands, his lips say something

—something the girl can't quite decode, except
she's fairly sure she likes it
and so suppresses the thought of those pop-up windows:

Some messages carry attachments that can harm
or destroy your system. Are you sure
this is from a trusted source?

She thinks, too, of all those online games
—all the times she's been owned. And owned others too.
She hearts this boy, but she's not sure
if she's *in heart* with him.

Beyond the car window, from the lookout, stars
of distant street-lamps glow brighter than the sky,
forming map-like constellations, all straight lines
and right angles, the grid system
a golden motherboard

from which they have unplugged
themselves, albeit briefly

letting fingers press messages
through fabric
into skin

pulsing
thrashing
wondering

what it means

FIVE: NAMELESS LOVES, ONE

Hatshepsut

Hatshepsut was the second historically confirmed female pharaoh

When she moves
I could mistake her for a lion,
weaving casual spirals as she twines
her long black beard round pale fingers,
the nails midnight blue
and gold.

We have been friends
since ancient times, through thousands
of skins, but always, she is the Pharoah,
the one who shines, and I
the servant girl,
hushed.

Her kohl-laced eyes
stare past me. Her tongue, lips, teeth
unravel anecdotes like scrolls
in hieroglyphs I long to trace
but can't: secrets of a maze
hers alone.

Now she tells me
how she's been thinking, lately
of a woman she once loved.

My face flushes.
I feign embarrassment.

The Immediacy of Forever

Red shoes,
skin dyed blue
by the bar lights, wrapped
in smoke like a loose silk robe,
you repeated my name

and repeated my name,
and I knew I'd never stop
repeating you repeating
my name, never stop
recalling your skin
under those lights,
dyed blue,
wrapped in smoke
like a silk robe,
loose

and I was right:
I never stopped
all these years
and still, I keep repeating
you repeating me,
keep reliving a right now
so long gone:

you
beneath the bar lights,
skin dyed blue,
red shoes.

Taking Time, part one, version two

It’s three weeks and four days
since this pandemic first began seeming like …
well, a pandemic.

By then, it was already a week
and six days since I last saw you,
since we last made love.

Afterwards, we lay in my bed
holding one another:
warm,
breathing,
wishing …

Then the farewell kiss,
the chill air,
hunger.

All I could think of was seeing you again.
I thought it would be a week.

The Official's neck bulges and quivers like the body of a silkworm surrounded by noisy schoolchildren—a classroom curiosity in a sealed-up box with a cling-wrap window and a few pinprick holes.

'Do you think I'm stupid? Hundreds of people come through here each day trying to fool me with phony details. I rarely hear anything as outrageous as this, though. Well come on, then, have you forged any papers for me?'

Naming the Tortoise, part five

As it continues glancing left and right, the tortoise seems sad, but not surprised. Its expression suggests confirmation of something expected but unwanted.

A tortoise this size must be centuries old, the child reflects. There can't be much it hasn't seen before. This thought brings a strange kind of calm: the child is tired of trying to explain things that don't make sense, to herself most of all.

Now a new thought unfolds, like a bud: the child knows better than to speak of the tortoise, to others, but what if she were to address it—speak to it? Does the tortoise have a voice? If so, what might it say?

You, Me, and Dora Maar

You wear red shoes to the Picasso exhibition.
I keep reminding myself, *Look at the art …*

Picasso never smiles in photographs
(appropriate for somebody so famous, so dead).
So many photographs. Dora's photographs.
This is her exhibition too.

Placards on the wall explain how they met
in a café, how she splayed one hand
on the table, and with the other danced a knife
round the crevices between gloved fingers
—a rabid, messy polka.

Picasso watched her stab and miss
and keep stabbing as her blood spilled and shone:
winking garnets, unflinching flesh.
He asked to keep the glove.

He painted her as a minotaur,
he painted her as a bird.
In a rare snap he catches her—Dora—off-guard:

small body, dark eyes staring into space.
She looks sad. She looks shy,
looks like half the girls who catch my train.
The cafe story doesn't seem possible.

Then I see you, spinning on the heels
of your winking red shoes.

So much is possible.

You are Dora Maar the Minotaur: strong,
sleek, shining creature of mystery and terror.
I am Dora Maar the bird: flightless, losing
myself in your labyrinth, wanting
yet afraid of you, ferocious you,
legendary, mythological, unknown.
We are funhouse mirrors and images,
kaleidoscope wormholes and dancing knives.
We are shadows, perpetually shifting,
changing and exchanging places. Now

I am Dora Maar the Minotaur: savage,
sweaty, and lost in my own maze. Invented,
outdated, a legend, a lie, slain and sliced up,
squealing at the sky where you, Dora Maar,
are wings spread, a wild bird, circling
above me, singing, sonorous,
weightless, wondrous,
out of reach.

You are painted blue but laughing,
rebuilding Guernica as a shiny silver egg.
You are dipping, diving, darting close
and far away (a brush of fabric,
we almost lock eyes …)

We are two women, so many women,
dancing careful art conversation:
proper as a white glove,
polished as a knife.

the train stops. shrill drone. doors part. MaggieMem beelines for the ladies', supporting her head with one white-knuckled hand tucked tight beneath her chin. this looks odd. but less odd than running through a crowded train station with no head.

after a minute or so of silent curses (waiting in line) MaggieMem finally stumbles into a cubicle. *thud* (the door). *cler-ick* (the lock). *sigh.* one-by-two metres of solitude. MaggieMem flops. cold plastic, damp, sticky against her thighs. she lets her head roll forward, rests it on her lap. bliss! sitting with one's head between one's knees, stockings down, bowels evacuating, not worrying what anybody thinks. her naked neck imagines a breeze, rejoices in momentary freedom from the burden of her head.

NAMELESS LOVE ONE / AUTO-CENTO FIVE

She is the Pharoah,
the one who shines,
skin dyed blue
by the bar lights.

Electronic music
repeats itself

—yeah yeah ooh baby
ooh yeah baby doll—

A pandemic:

things
don't make sense.
She looks sad. She looks shy.
So much is possible.
Perhaps she is searching for words …

sense

motion. emotion. waves, moons
stars. dancing.

Hungry
for treasure

—a gun?

I can't believe she is doing this.
For fuck's sake.

I dreamed—

Sensing / Making, version five

sense.

sense the dictionary. sense wisdom,
motion. emotion. waves, moons
stars. dancing.

sense experience, sense connection.

sense cards. houses. halls, malls, cemeteries.
the world opened wide.
deep. Time.

sense beehives, the undressed ocean, foam feathers beating.
across mountains of quiet. Time.

sense

wide, then wider—

I dreamed—

Island, part one, version two

I am the island.
Sometimes I am kind.
Sometimes I lash out.

Stubborn Selkirks
and yearning Crusoes come hungry
for treasure,
but they don't find it.

I am not a man. I am not a woman.
I have no name. My name is I.

Yes,
amongst all these men there came a woman.

I made myself lush for her,
provided all she could want.

Too much, I suspect.

My tree-arms ached with the weight of ripe fruits,
left to rot. She preferred meat,
set about capturing my forests.

She had a gun. The bullets tore.

In secret, I wept. Still,
I continued giving.

I let her—
I let her—

She cultivated me.

Then, one day she climbed to the top of my bluff,
stood surveying the land she had shaped.

Damn you, island. I liked you better wild.

Small Talk

I can't believe she is doing this
in Brunswick St, of all places.
Crema clings to her lips as she weaves them,
winds them, teases and twines them,
long lean muscles stretching fluid and obscene
into shapes—such shapes—
I gasp.

Still she pushes them onto me,
forges them into me,
these shapes,
her shapes,
her lips
her words.

She is an alchemist, mixing precious metals with her tongue.
Her mouth contorts, casually ominous cloud
pouring out more of them,
more of them—words.

Long words. Slow words. Strange words. New words.
Words with syllables strung sleek and shining
Sudden words. Foreign words.
Spice-Spiked Four-Letter words.
Soft, sharp, bitter, sweet, latte-laced words.

She strips words, shaves them, parades them pink
and shining. Drizzles them like hot wax
into the curved flesh hollows of my ears.
She makes words take to themselves
with blunt objects, makes them ache
and bleed new meaning.

She splits words open, makes them gape
like pomegranates. She reaches in,
explores, discovers, leans across the table
and feeds me

words …

I speak:
deformed fish flee my lips
in a fury of salt stung sounds
(I was not raised to make such noise!)

She is the fisher, casting lines down my throat
and hauling up diamonds, dirty uncut diamonds:
diamonds I've swallowed, words I've swallowed,
words I don't want to say. She is hauling them out,
dragging jagged fragments from my soft oesophagus.
until I can't stop:

I spew
all over the trendy silver table, I spew
fish I spew shit I spew blood I spew diamonds I spew
words
words
words
words
(&*()&*^(&*^&^%%$*^$$#@
$#%$%&*&*^%%$$#%^&*&*^&^&%$#%$^&**^%^%$%
$#$@#@!$%%^%^^&&)&*^&*%^%$%$#@##$%^^&&*)
^&%^%^%$%$#@#$%%^&&&*^&%^%^%$%$$##$%^%
^&*^&&&((^&*%^&$

and more words

till the table is covered—
sugar pot, salt, pepper, phones, bags, keys, coffee cups,
both of us covered

(the waiter offers a napkin; I dab my chin.)

Meanwhile
two men at a nearby table sip lattes
talking amongst themselves, as if all this were normal
and everyday
and—as I keep telling myself it really is—

nothing
more
than a conversation.

Through the Cracks, version five

At two, three, four a.m., I'd trace the fingers of one hand over the bumpy knuckles of my other and know I wasn't totally adrift.

Trix detergent—sometimes lavender, sometimes lemon—
Calming.

I hadn't really planned, at twenty-one, to be living with a boyfriend—especially not after just two months.

For fuck's sake.

You're making the wine glasses cloudy.

After that I made sure
Trav didn't complain again.

He was passed out a lot of the time.
Bliss: staring through the window, thinking

If we pooled enough people with enough mixed-up plate sets, we'd be able to sort all the stray pieces into matching sets. Then everybody could take a set home and our kitchens, our lives would be like new.

Except

what I wanted

I knew.

SIX: NAMELESS LOVES, TWO

Taking Time, part one, version one

It's three weeks and four days since I touched another human. Touched anybody, in any way. Since then, nothing. No hugs, no handshakes, no high fives. Not even that elbow-bump manoeuvre people were doing when this pandemic first began seeming like … well, a pandemic. By then, it was already a week and six days since I last saw you. Since we last made love. Afterwards, we lay in my bed holding one another: warm, breathing, me wishing you could stay but understanding when you said, *Yes, but these things take time*. Then the farewell kiss by your car, the chill air priming my hunger for the heat in your lips, your skin. All I could think of was seeing you again. I thought it would be a week, which seemed an age, but what could we do? You were busy. I was busy. We were two busy women, striving to juggle appointments, meet deadlines, slay to-do lists, and around the edges of all that, seize moments to meet and explore whatever we might have been becoming, together.

How to Get Inside an Orange

Step one: surrender your knife.
Recall your fingertips,
the heirlooms they carry.
Your ancestors dug shelters
and gasped at fires.
You have thirty-two teeth, give or take.
You have more hair than you let grow.
You have dreams in which you grasp
the trick of flying. You forget
and keep forgetting
each time you wake.
Step two: close your eyes

and tear skin. A chasm.
Open. Let yourself fall.
There may be a stinging sensation.
It's acid, after all. Like wine.
Step three: suck

the amniotic, spit
yourself out
of yourself. Clean. Step
four: break

into sections, each
made of sections.
Step five: the centre, a seed:

will you be the soil?

Hungry, part six

The Official speaks too fast. The woman catches only one word. She sobs.

'I'm not Stupid! I'm Hungry!'

'Fine, fine. Let's skip it for now. What about your second name?'

The woman stares blankly.

'I'm just Hungry. Nothing but Hungry. I don't like it any more than you do. I want to change. I want to be New. New Begin.'

Through the Cracks, version six

They were all similar,
and none precisely the same—

flowers faded,
pieces missing,
the cracks suggested stories,
lent an inadvertent wabi sabi quality

—individuality, artfulness,
purpose, truth—

to see through the cracks felt like crawling inside
a place dark and warm and safe:

brokenness spoke of ways to fit.

THE PORNOGRAPHY IN CLOUDS

We went to the drive in
at sunrise, parked to face
a tomorrow that was already today.
You unlocked my skin
and I flew out, wings rejoicing, eager
to dance with breezes,
meet storms in the eye.
The sun was a raw egg
we smashed open, sank inside.
We were pink ants
drowning in fire.

Naming the Tortoise, part six

The child draws a breath. Yes. She has decided. She will address the tortoise. At last.

'You pick strange times to come visit,' the child remarks, trying to sound offhand and casual, like this is all no big deal. 'Don't you know it's night-time? That's when people sleep. Don't you sleep? Aren't you tired?'

The tortoise makes a wriggle that could be a nod.

'My name is Anna,' the child ventures. 'Do you have a name?'

The tortoise wriggles again.

'Hmmm. I thought it was that. Hey, look. I need to pee. Real bad. You won't hurt me if I kind of creep round you to get to the bathroom—will you?'

The tortoise flares its nostrils, offended yet still unsurprised.

Nameless Love two / Auto-cento six

Close your eyes,
let yourself fall:

another human

—explore—

dance with breezes,
meet storms in the eye

—do you think I'm stupid?

Used to think
I knew nothing. Yes.

You won't hurt me
—will you?

Danger has a sweet sting.
It's always sunrise.

Running through a crowded train station
with no head.

Common and uncommon dreams
recurring differently—

You grabbed my hand, made me feel—

Too much, I suspect.

Small Questions too Daft to Ask

How do you plot the circumference of a sunrise?
All those shades of orange,
what's their molecular structure?
Their atomic weight?
Where can I dig up the square root of wanting?
The final point in the remainder of a dream?

Danger has a sweet sting: would it stain the litmus violet?
What's the carbon content of a scream?
Love equals hate to the power of Y, but what is Y? And why
does the subtraction of loss equal the addition of nothing?
At what degree Celsius does human blood become steam?

Two people complete the same equation,
arrive at different answers, both true, though incorrect.
The common denominators:
birth
and breaking.

For is breath not dying's inverse?
Why must we keep splitting the atom of I?

You'll tell me Why and I'll say *But Why?*

Every new day is an unknown formula,
the volume of each moment infinite, yet ever swallowed
by the next—and the next

in greedy ripples. It's always sunrise.

how lovely it would be if MaggieMem didn't have to worry about her head! she could tote it in a snazzy bag or display it on her desk. no more piggybacking this obese secret. she could be so efficient. but this is a futile dream. after all, MaggieMem works in PR. an industry utterly unprepared to tolerate a woman with a disobedient head. she is the front-desk receptionist. she likes the smell of white-out in the mornings.

MaggieMem's Mother laments this lack of success. it wouldn't be so bad if MaggieMem were Married-With-Or-Working-On-Kids. but MaggieMem is NotMarried.NoProspects. and MaggieMem is AlmostThirty (has been AlmostThirty since she was NoLongerTwentyOne).

Sensing / Making, version six

There was sense in senses of judgement.
Then there was the sensuous, and sensing.

Sound. Taste. Touch. Smell. Sight. Fright. Lust. Emotion.

Waves, tides, rises. Moons and stars. Rhythms
and dancing. Intuition—connection.

Moments snatched from dreams. Fragile. Detailed. Trembling.

Opened wide. Undressed.
Hearts beating. Danced and danced, sharing gifts.

Then rushed a tide.

You Made Me Run Down Dark Streets

You made me run through dark streets
at four a.m. Your laughter
was as zig zag as your name
as the sentences you ran together
like song loops on a strobe lit floor

One strand of hair escaped bleach and scissors,
fell over your left eye, a reminder of that girl
you might have been, before—

You grabbed my hand, made me feel
the way it must have felt for those men
who bought me drinks when I was eighteen.

You were only eighteen.

And I was nineteen, barely older.
But you made me feel ancient
and at the same time, a child
like I'd lived all that life already dead
and not yet born.

You were eighteen, yet so old with your lips
and so old in moments you thought unseen
when you slipped from your smile
like a pair of too-tight stockings.

You made me run through dark streets
at four a.m. Your laughter
was as zig zag as your name.

Island, part one, version one

I am the island. Sailors wreck themselves upon me. I do not invite them. I do not ask that they leave. Sometimes none come for ages and ages. I cannot say how long. Time is their invention, not mine. I remain silent, as always, never still. My forests grow and die. Beasts breed and battle within me. I spurt lava from high peaks and hidden aqueducts, sizzle and reshape myself. These things do not stop happening just because nobody sees or records.

Sometimes I am kind, providing fresh streams, nourishment, buried treasure, exotic delights. Sometimes I lash out with storms and predators, offering nothing but barren rocks and thistles for shelter from the night. Still, they come to me, these stubborn Selkirks and yearning Crusoes. They come hungry, half-naked, half-clothed in the delusions it was their skill, not the surf, that swept them ashore. They come for adventure, decrying the dullness of their homelands, their mothers, those safe and sensible lives. Having escaped the known, they then rebuild it as frantically as they can. Frightened of the darkness in my perfectly good caves, they fell my forests and gut my mountains to fashion houses. They chip time's notches into my tree trunks, my limbs. They try to make a mother of me. They are frightened of my caves, my fire-pools. There is treasure everywhere, but they don't find it. They don't know how to look. At the first opportunity, they cry S.O.S. and race home, yearning to re-clothe themselves, to reclaim everything from which they said they wanted to cast themselves away.

I am not a man. I am not a woman. Countries are referred to with the pronoun she, but I am no country. I have no name. My name is I. I am land, unmapped, unowned. I shift shape, break off, float, resurface, reassign myself ever shifting co-ordinates. Sometimes I am tropical, sometimes cold. I am no particular island. I am the island, the only one of many. I am five-million fictions, one flaking rock of fact. And yes, amongst all these men there came one Crusoe who was a woman.

The men came fleeing from their mothers, but she came fleeing from the men. She wasn't frightened of my caves. Darkness was the very thing she sought. Her feet were soft upon my sand in a way I'd never felt before. I wanted her to walk and walk and walk. So I did what I don't often do: I made myself lush for her, provided all she could want, and more. Too much, I suspect. My tree-arms ached with the weight of ripe fruits, most of which were left to rot. She preferred meat and set about capturing the wild beasts in my forests. She had a gun. The bullets tore me every time. In secret, I wept, pooling tears in underground springs. Still, the feel of her feet on my sand remained worth whatever else she did. So I continued giving. Safety, warmth, shelter, food, birdsong, beauty. Life. I let her build huts in places where I would once have showered avalanches. I let her topple trees and plough fields. She cultivated me, carved shapes, planted new flora and released fauna that bred uninhibited. I was loathe to so much as sweep her footprints from my shore. Then one day she climbed to the top of my bluff and stood surveying the land she had shaped.

Damn you, island. I liked you better wild.

INTERMISSION

Sometimes there's nothing
for it but to go
climb a mountain

—find some other side
from which to come
down

SEVEN: NAMELESS LOVES, THREE

ISLAND, PART TWO, VERSION ONE

Damn you, island. I liked you better wild.

Her words bounced and echoed between cut-grass valleys and craters where my flames had all but petered out. Her words were bullets. They ricocheted, cratering my cliff-face. A rumbling ensued. The bluff was sandstone. It might have crumbled there and then. But I held the shockwaves. I breathed in, breathed out. Yes, islands breathe. Of course we do. The tide was coming in. It wiped her footprints from my shore.

I waited until she had climbed down to her hut. Let her think I wouldn't react. I was still deciding if I should. She fell asleep, but as the night wore on her words were still shaking inside my soil. Finally I couldn't take it. I let go. Let go of everything I'd been holding onto for her sake, let it fall from the sky in fat, sharp splatters. For months I'd only rained just the right amount to feed her crops, when in fact I was capable of so much more. I pelted in through the roof of her shabby shelter, blew it apart like a snickering wolf. She screamed. She was shivering, wide awake, naked.

You want wild? I'll give you wild.

I washed away her fields, dropped branches to kill her feral pets, zapped lightening bolts just inches from the box where she kept the powder for that damn gun she loved so much.

I kept the storm raging until morning. Then, relenting, I offered sunshine to warm her bare skin. I sent a gentle breeze through the branches of the pomegranate tree, coaxing one ripe red globe to fall and roll down from its bluff to settle beside her on the beach. She ignored the gift, ate nothing. And she wouldn't stop shivering, not even when I made the air gloriously warm. She sobbed all morning, all afternoon. Why? I only gave her what she asked. She sobbed for days and days, though I kept the season perfect.

I longed for her to re-sew her fields, to walk with her soft feet on my shore. But she remained huddled, said nothing. Then one day a plane flew overhead. Flying it was a man. She rolled over, spread her legs towards the sky.

S.O.S.

The man in the plane swooped down. He flung out a ladder. She climbed. She climbed. Into his arms. He clasped her, pulled her in. They disappeared. Back to safety. Back to the comfortable life from which she'd fled.

And me? I continued growing and dying, my beasts battling, breeding. That's what islands do.

You're Missing

They're everywhere I go now—holes

where you're not,
things I don't hear
because you're not here
to say them,
words stuck in my throat
without your ears
to catch them
like your arms aren't here
to catch me
and your lips—

your lips were so warm.

In the supermarket, I reach
towards—

then pause,
withdraw.
Even saving money stings
when it's because you're not coming round

In time, I'll sew them up—these holes—
re-fill them like I have before with others.

But for now, missing you
is a way to keep you
here.

Sensing / Making, version seven

told, wanted, tried—sought
snatched, decided, hoped, turned, built
—took

Stood. Waited. Trembling.

opened,
drew, blew, said—

tried.

went, gathered
stewed, cried, spat,
grimaced, undressed, made—

would not.

grew,
clipped, busted, ground,
made, looked, refused,
rode, slept, ate, starved, sat
danced, came, danced, left,
tried, remained, turned, stopped, asked—

opened, rushed.

Marilyn and the Electric Chair

You knocked unexpected, barged
in sporting a Pablo Picasso haircut
and Andy Warhol eyes. You sat down.
You were Marilyn. And the electric chair.
You were Marilyn crapping on the electric chair.
You crapped your truth all over my lounge room.

Your truth was a baby
with screams for eyes.
Your truth was Tupperware
and Sunday papers
and many things.

I wasn't one of them.

I stood back and took it
like the man I could never be
to make you happy.

My ears swallowed sounds, words.
My head nodded. My throat said, *fine.*

Hungry, part seven

'You want to change your name?' The Official queries in a yawning monotone.

She nods her head, exuberant.

'Yes! Yes! New!'

'Then I must see your papers.'

She tilts her head sideways, squinting at The Official. Then, as though something has clicked, she forages in her pocket and produces a filthy notebook.

Nameless Love three / Auto-cento seven

I liked you better wild.

Your lips
they were
so warm.

The world opened wide

—beehives, the undressed ocean, foam feathers beating—

then wider.

You were Marilyn. And the electric chair.

New. Begin.
Softness and warmth
in a place rough and cold

at two, three, four a.m.
—Bliss:

not worrying what anybody thinks.
Learn to breathe. In. And. Out. Falling

from the top floor, never hitting the ground.
Still, it stung.

Naming the Tortoise, part seven

The tortoise wriggles to one side, clearing as much corridor as it can for the child to get past. Not much. A tight space. But the tortoise can't help that. It's a huge thing in a tiny house. All space is tight.

Again, the child draws breath. Lets it go. Draws it again. To hesitate any longer will be rude, she knows. Creeping forth, she attempts to tip-toe around the tortoise without touching. She sucks her stomach in, moves as carefully as she can. At the same time, she wants to move fast. The nervousness and chill night air have made her muscles tight. Her body feels not quite her own.

A floorboard creaks. The child starts, swaying to steady herself. Her hand brushes against the tortoise—its leg, not its shell. She is shocked to discover softness and warmth in a place she aways imagined would be so rough and cold. A realisation floods in: this creature's body flows with blood, like her own. If cut, it would bleed, would feel pain, like her own.

The child's eyes meet those of the tortoise. Burnt out stars. Then she feels her bladder seizing. If she doesn't move, she really will lose control. Breaking the tortoise's gaze, she scurries for the bathroom. Thrusting the door shut, she hitches up her nightie and plonks upon the seat. It's cold, colder than the floor, but she doesn't care. She's made it. Safe. At least for now. The piss flows and flows and flows. Then something else flows too. From her eyes, tears. From her lungs and lips, muffled sobs.

Through the Cracks, version seven

At Clauscen Street
I felt
filthy,
out of order.

In the Melbourne winter,
I got chilblains.

One thing
was useful
—lavender.

Our plates
were chipped,

beer stains on the carpet,

I let him rave and feel justified.

I was small,
faded,
missing,
cracked.

I used to think
I knew
Nothing.

In truth
I knew
I didn't like being called stupid

THE WOMAN WITH THE DISOBEDIENT HEAD, PART SEVEN

MaggieMem might have achieved more if not for her head. if MaggieMem's head were normal, MaggieMem might be InCharge of the PR firm. and Married. or at least WithProspects. but MaggieMem has a disobedient head. though she manages to keep it in place most of the time, MaggieMem will always have a disobedient head. whether she was born with it or developed it as a result of some trauma remains a topic of debate.

MaggieMem's family have decided that MaggieMem has a disobedient head because MaggieMem has a disobedient head.

the severity fluctuates. sometimes her glue holds for months on end: for phases, MaggieMem almost forgets to be frightened. then there are phases where absolutely nothing can hold things in place. always, at any moment, MaggieMem can come unstuck. sometimes the cause is obvious: MaggieMem has taken on too much, put herself under stress or indulged in irresponsible behaviour. other times—like today—there is no clear explanation, no warning.

MaggieMem's head comes unstuck because MaggieMem's head comes unstuck.

The Science of Breathing Out

Pilates class is full of middle-class women
with blonde bobs and cake stall smiles.
I want the weights room. Want the fever stink
of testosterone, the grunting Darwinism of it all.
Want the air to prickle with *What are you doing here?*
Want to saunter because *I'll do as I please.*

But no, not today.
The trainer said I need Pilates
so I can learn to breathe. In. And Out.
What's hard about breathing? I wonder.
Then I try and I can't.

Relax your ribs, the teacher tells us.
My ribs are bone. This is stupid, I want to say,
but my throat is bone too. My lungs, my skin, my face
all bone. I'm a scowl-faced carving.
I've forgotten how to gasp, to hum, to set free
all the stagnant air I've gorged.

How can emptiness take so much space?

You Told Me Your Name

and I took it, held it
on my tongue, giddy as vodka
infused with sherbet: everything
good about childhood,
poured into a glass the shape of dying.
You told me your name

and I swallowed it in one go
like the seed of a chocolate watermelon.
I wanted it to grow. You
told me your name
and it was the only name ever heard,
the only sound. It was falling

from the top floor, never hitting the ground,
an unlived memory, a beautiful wound.
Your name. You told me
and I tattooed it on my lungs,
let it become the breath
I couldn't catch, every word never said.

As you tip-toed out the front door,
while I stood, half-dressed, still
half dreaming. You told me
your name, but not your number.

It took two black coffees and all day
to remember my own

Taking Time, part two, version one

You started isolating early because of that cold you caught. Plus your asthma. Last year you had a collapsed lung. Still, it stung when you said you wouldn't see me. I understood. I understand. You could die. But still. But still. That last time together, we'd discussed moving in—at the end of the year, if we were still going well. Are we still going well? Are we going at all? We message. We video-chat. But I can't feel you, can't breathe you, can't sense the things your breath and heartbeat would tell me of all you can't tell me, because words are but one language. Yesterday, out walking, I saw a father hug his child. Tears flowed behind my dark glasses. What happens to bodies—chemically and hormonally—when starved of touch for weeks? Months? Years? I recall an old textbook: a monkey with its metal mother, pre-research ethics. They don't put animals through that anymore. My mother phoned yesterday. Her tone was strained. It's twenty years since I first told her I was bi, but she never believed me, not with the others. Something in how I speak of you is different. She gets it now. She's shattered, but she gets it. I wanted to introduce you two. She said, *Yes, but these things take time.*

EIGHT: A CROOKED MAGIC, ONE

Dia / Gnosis

It's a crooked kind of magic—this fine art
of a science.
Dia, as in diagonal
(slanting/sloping/oblique/transverse/crossing over …)
diagram
(a map, a graph, a chart … putting things on paper …)
or dialling
(phoning, calling)

and gnosis, as in knowledge
and knowing, especially of things unknown,
perhaps un/knowable.

Hence the magic
and the slant—the crooks
and crannies—the crossings
over, under, around
and through—the marks
and markings
that map things and make them
markable, subject
to remark.

This magic calls and summons,
slices and tears, breaks and remakes
what it promises
to heal

Marked

At fifteen I lost my voice:

I had a sore throat—fever—shakes—
and so I went to the doctor, symptoms scribbled
on a pocketed scrap of paper.

He—the doctor—called me in
and gestured: chair. I sat, obedient, waiting
to be asked why I was there. Instead,
So what
shall we do
about that acne?

Then he was scribbling a script, tearing
it from his pad, and I was out
in the corridor, blinking
at his prescription—a cure that made me sick.

The paper was so white, clean, corners
crisp, the etched-in signature so
official: a legislation, judgement, a decree.

Pocketing it, I discovered the other paper:
the symptoms my doctor never saw.
Had he thought it odd
that through the whole consult
I spoke not one word?

Or was that to be expected
from a girl marked as I was?

Island, part two, version two

I liked you better wild.

Her words ricocheted.
The bluff might have crumbled there and then,
but I held

—breathed in, breathed out—

The tide was coming.

I waited,
deciding if I should. Finally
I let go
of everything,
blew apart like a snickering wolf.

Shivering, wide awake, naked.

You want wild? I'll give you wild.

Lightening bolts.
That damn gun.
I kept the storm raging until morning.

Then, sunshine to warm her,
a gentle breeze,
the pomegranate tree,
one ripe red globe.

She ignored the gift, shivering,
even when I made the air gloriously warm.

She sobbed.

Why?

She sobbed for days and days,
remained huddled, said nothing.

S.O.S.

A ladder.
She climbed.
She climbed
back to the life from which she'd fled.

And me? I continued.
That's what islands do.

Sensing / Making, version eight

mouth, *make sense—*
manufacture Sound. Taste. Touch. Smell.
Lust. Love. Experience. Knowing.

piece together something—
make something
make sense

please, *Try*

.......................buzzzz

Try again,

foam mouth,
busted tiny beating mouth,
starved mouth,
closed mouth.

a Crooked Magic one / Auto-cento eight

A map, a graph, a chart … putting things on paper …
so white, clean, corners crisp.

You want wild? I'll give you wild.

Knowledge.
Trembling.
A tide,
yawning—

Yes! Yes!

Skies and oceans, eyes and sapphires, petals,
ink, plastic lids of pens—don't chew.

Bruises. Planets. Marbles. Blood.

This will make you feel warmer.
Hang on. I'll fetch a glass.

The oyster is gone, and in its place,
a collapsed lung—metal mother—

the smell of white-out
and mortgages.

Hungry, part eight

'This is paper. My only paper. It's precious to me, but I'll give to you if that's what this takes.'

The woman pushes the notebook through a slot beneath The Official's window. It is a specially designed slot: one which will accept items, but never offer nor return them. There is another slot hidden at the back of the box, through which items can freely pass both ways, but it is locked at present, covered in cobwebs.

The Official accepts the notebook, handling it as if cautious of disease. Its pages are stained and crinkled, covered with smudged inky scribblings. Every few pages or so these is a gap and then something that looks like a date. The dates go back further than this woman could have been alive. Periodically, the size and slant of the scribblings change: more than one hand has added to this book. It is very thick, and, though old, less than half-way full.

Blue, version two

The first blue I knew was blood.

Later there would be skies and oceans,
eyes and sapphires, petals, ink, plastic lids
of pens my teachers said, don't chew.
The skin-ripple of a hushed tattoo.

The blue of singers, songs, the sounds
and shoes, jeans, dresses, uniforms
I wore reluctantly, eyeliner brandished with glee.
There would be bruises. Planets. Marbles.

But first, the blood.
When we cut ourselves we rust.
A kind of blossoming, a bloom
of buds unfolding just to die.

We are fields of roses, yes,
in lips and finger tips, the speckled light.
We could not be fire were we not also smoke.
Could not be red without the blue.

The first blue I knew was living.
The first blue I knew was blood.

Naming the Tortoise, part eight

Returning from the toilet, the child peers up and down the hallway. The tortoise remains where it was, its shell and eyes as huge as ever.

'Are you hungry?' the child asks. 'Is that why you're here?'

The tortoise remains wordless, but the child is learning languages of silence, and so pads her way to the kitchen. The tortoise follows. In darkness, the child shifts a chair and climbs aboard to reach above the fridge. There she finds and pulls down the cardboard box her parents store there, the one filled with the sweet red liquid that makes the world light and floating. The liquid that helps with forgetting things it's bad to remember—things like what the child saw (but didn't see) before she first saw the tortoise.

'You're cold, I'll bet,' the child comments. 'This will make you feel warmer. Hang on. I'll fetch a glass.'

Mistaking Judith Butler for a Self-help Guru

My body is an oyster shell.
The doctor taps it with her pen,
purses her lips at the dull, hollow echo.
Prising it open, she confirms
what we both already knew:
the oyster is gone, and in its place, pearls,
a whole string, long enough to hang an infant.

I exit the doctor's office, swaying,
unsteady, I have slipped
off the rails of a set track called womanhood
and find myself in some no man's land.
No, man, not mad. Not woman
but still no man … *noman* … nomad?

Is this exile? Or liberation
from the children I never wanted,
the mother I was terrified I'd be. At last, now I ask,
what can I be—

come?

Dangling in the space
this question opens, I find myself
if nothing else, far from alone.

There are so many of us.
Not gender's undoings, rather proof

gender was and is
from the start, always undoing and undone.

Taking Time, part two, version two

You started isolating early—
that cold you caught,
your asthma,
last year, a collapsed lung.

Still, it stung
—you wouldn't see me.

I understood. I understand.
But still. But still.

That last time together, we'd discussed—

—at the end
of the year, if we were still going well.

Are we? Are we?
I can't feel, can't breathe.

Tell me
all you can't tell me.
Words are but one language.

Yesterday, out walking, I saw a father hug his child.
Tears flowed behind my dark glasses.
I recall an old textbook: a monkey with its metal mother.
They don't put animals through that anymore.
My mother never believed me, not with the others.
I wanted to introduce you two.

Yes, but these things take time.

from the corner of a bleary, glue-smudged eye, MaggieMem notices the time. blast. she needs to get moving. MaggieMem does not wish to place her head upon a public toilet floor. nor does she wish to hold it while she wipes herself. she lays a little mattress of toilet paper and rests it down—ever so gently—taking care it doesn't roll under the door. the next complication: how to wash her hands? MaggieMem was a girl scout. she has a stash of antibacterial wipes in her handbag. she also has some dental floss and a sewing kit. somewhere. MaggieMem's handbag is huge and filled with junk. right now she can't see a thing. (well, actually, she can see the toilet floor and the underpants round the ankles of a woman in the cubicle next door, but this doesn't help). holding the bag open with her left hand, she scoops up her head in her right and squints into the black leather abyss of crumpled dockets, broken-lid lippies, forgotten phone numbers and poorly-wrapped wads of spent gum. finally, she locates what she needs.

Through the Cracks, version eight

It was just what I felt like doing.
I got chilblains, but they were worth it:
I wasn't totally adrift.

Our plates resembled the set my parents owned
when I was small: warm, wonderful flower plates.

I wept,
I wept,

making glasses cloudy,

made sure to clean up the mess
—right parts in their rightful order—

the dishwater made me feel warm.

NINE: A CROOKED MAGIC, TWO

it is very hard to sew one-handed without looking. not to mention the sting. MaggieMem grits her teeth. time is ticking. the dental floss dances a clumsy green polka round her pale neck. very tacky. though it smells better than glue. she dons a thick black scarf. rather odd for the middle of summer. it will probably raise speculation about MaggieMem's social life. at AlmostThirty she still can't decide whether to like or hate such attention. if only turtlenecks would come into fashion.

after a mad dash through the city, a sweaty, subtly spearmint scented MaggieMem slides into the reception desk. only one minute late. her neck itches but she doesn't scratch it. she smooths an imaginary crinkle in her shirt. then gasps. something cold and slimy on the side of her head. blast. she should have checked while she had the chance. but no. rushrushrush. she feigns casual indifference as the wet thing slides down her neck, settles sticky in the folds of her scarf. slippery slick, bulbous as a slug. MaggieMem's ear. she waits until no one is looking then fishes it out and stuffs it in her handbag. if she keeps her hair forward nobody will notice. lucky it's the left ear. MaggieMem favours telephone calls with her right. just as she zips up her handbag, MaggieMem recalls the poorly wrapped wads of gum. too late. now MaggieMem has gum in her ear. she sighs. this sort of thing would never happen to her Mother.

Blue, version one

The first blue I knew was blood.

Later there would be skies and oceans,
eyes and sapphires, petals, ink, plastic lids
of pens my teachers said, *don't chew*,
the slight skin-ripple of a hushed tattoo.

There would be blue the way of feeling
and blues the songs, the singers, sounds
somehow able to make me feel *less blue*,
and more crucially, to make me feel.

There would be blue jelly, shiny, quivering,
blue shoes, jeans, dresses, uniforms I wore
reluctantly, eyeliner I brandished with glee.
There would be bruises. Planets. Marbles.

Stars and other blue things. Endless
shades of navy, azure, cobalt, turquoise, topaz,
aquamarine … debates over where blue ends
and violet begins (not to mention green …)

There would be rumours: some can't see it,
in nature, we shouldn't eat it. Forget red:
blue is the ultimate warning sign,
the labelled poison that glows, alluring.

But before that, there was just blue
as blue, and blue was blood. Blue blood.
I'm not talking aristocratic lineages.
Believe me, I'm anything but.

I'm talking the truths our skins tell us
when vessels burst beneath surfaces,
when we trace the branching trajectories
of those highways in our wrists.

Blood is blue. Even if it's not. Science tell us
blood is red, always red—albeit darker,
duller shades when starved
of the oxygen that stokes its fires.

For we are rivers, mineral springs
flowing with iron. When we are cut
or cut ourselves—when our blood spills
and mingles with air—we rust:

A kind of blossoming, an opening
into brief brilliance, like blooms
on buds unfolding purely to die
and so become alive again.

But even before this, blood is red, always.
It's just tricks of light that turn us blue.
For blue light reflects more easily than red,
dances faster from flesh to eye. Yet

This makes us no less blue than the sky
—which, like roses, comes in many colours.
The same pigment that tints roses red
paints cornflowers too. Hydrangeas shift lilac

to pink, depending on pH. So, we are hydrangeas.
We are fields and fields of roses—red, it's plain
to see in lips and fingertips, in the flushes
that light quiet breasts in fervent moments.

But like a jazz upswing, we could not be fire
were we not also smoke—could not be red
without the idea, at least, of blue. This
is the song I sing myself on days that outswing

Blue: days of grey—days I need in order to see,
smell and taste colour all over again.

Heroin makes you blue, a friend once said.
Neither of us laughed. It wasn't funny.

The fist blue I knew was living.
The first blue I knew was blood.

The Official's nose screws into a snort.

'I mean your identification papers.'

'Identity,' the woman nods, pointing through the glass at the notebook she has surrendered.

The Official's nose screws some more.

'Birth certificate. Driver's license. A bank letter or a phone bill … '

She nods her head wildly, smiles, and claps her hands.

'Yes! Please. Those are just the things I need.'

'No, no, no. I can't give them to you unless you give them to me. How can I give you an identity if I cannot confirm your legitimate identity?'

A Crooked Magic two / Auto-cento nine

The severity fluctuates:

brief brilliance, like blooms
on buds unfolding purely to die
and so become alive again

too faded, too many pieces
missing or cracked

S.O.S.

Growing and dying—that's what islands do.

Stained and crinkled,
smudged inky scribblings—a body

with hands and arms and legs and toes and breath—

one foot and then the other and the other and the other and the other and No No No Oh No

—can't feel, can't breathe, can't sense—

They don't put animals through that anymore.

The light switches on:

songs, sounds,

blue, blue—

They say there are things
that can take this away

But tomorrow, the wind may wake again

Island, part two, version three

Damn you. I liked you.

Her words were bullets,
cratering my cliff-face.

I breathed in, breathed out.
The tide wiped her footprints from my shore.

I waited.
She fell asleep.
The night wore on.

I couldn't take it. I let go,
blew apart.

You want wild?

I kept raging until morning.
Then, relenting, I offered a pomegranate.

She ignored the gift,
sobbed all morning, all afternoon

Why?
she asked.

I said nothing.

Then, a plane,
a man.

S.O.S.

He flung out a ladder.
She climbed.

His arms clasped her, pulled her in.

Growing and dying,
that's what islands do.

Blue, version three

blood,
skies, oceans
eyes, sapphires,
hushed tattoo,

songs, sounds,
uniforms,
eyeliner,
bruises, planets, marbles

—when we cut ourselves we rust—

blossoming,
unfolding

lips and finger tips,
fire
red

—first blue
—first blue

Through the Cracks, version nine

I should try be nice, clean, new again.

Hot water is a nice thing, chilblains worth it
at two, three, four a.m.

Adrift in detergent, I could have been
what I should be
in this moment—and the next—and the next—

Warm, wonderful.

I think I thought I liked liking the cracks—
being the one to see beauty inside brokenness.

I get sick making sure not to complain,
thinking things never said aloud
because who would I say them to?

Sometimes I know.

Taking Time, part two, version three

You started isolating

—cold—
it stung.

You wouldn't see me.
I understood. I understand. But still. But still.

That last time together—
Are we still going?

I can't feel, can't breathe, can't—words
are but one language.

Yesterday, tears
behind my dark glasses.
They don't put animals through that anymore.

My mother phoned,
her tone strained.
It's twenty years since—

She never believed me, not with the others.
Something in you is different.

She gets it now.
shattered,
but she gets it.

She said, *Yes, but take time.*

Naming the Tortoise, part nine

Footsteps in the corridor. The light switches on. The child's father stands in his dressing gown, brow furrowed.

'What are you doing?'

'It's for the tortoise.'

'The tortoise?'

The child points. Her father doesn't look.

'There's no tortoise.'

'But there is.'

The child's father draws a long slow breath, exhaling slowly, as though the air hurts his body.

'Anna, we've been through this before. There's no tortoise.'

Remembering My Lithium Body

Remembering a body with hands
that shook and arms
that shook and legs and toes and breath

always shaking, a body
with nerves all plugged up, muddied
by salt
and salt
and salt

in every synapse, a body
with a salty, metal cunt
anaesthetised,
amputated,
torn, a body, walking
barely

one foot and then the other and the other and the other and the other and

like a bride, drowned
in white, washed clean, wiped out
of world and self, yet still, a body

forgotten but not gone, a body
shaking, tectonic, waiting, a dormant body
that after two years woke
and from its mouth spewed

No No No Oh No

a body that was lucky
someone heard.

Blue Again

Blue, today is blue
but not lonely, nor cold.
No black dogs haunt this corner.

Rather, pigeons—soft,
cooing, huddled,
sharing warmth.

I am one of them,
feathers melting into feathers
melting into open
stairwell
skies.

They say there are things
that can take this away,
but why should I want that?

I'm already still soaring,
dipping spinning remembering
all the other sides of all those clouds
the cautious friends said, *don't touch.*

Tomorrow, the wind may wake again, and then …

But for now, blue is no bad colour for becoming
in the shadows of a bleached white world.

Sensing / Making, version nine

mouth—please—how

—no recipe—

dreams recurring differently

—make something from them?

words—cards—houses—malls—cemeteries
—a world?

ears—beehives—their buzz—the ocean—sheets of foam
—a bed—lie down?

wings—limbs—feathers—bones—hearts—beaches
—mountains—sun—Time—loss—everything

mouth—*What? How?*

TEN: MEANWHILE BACK IN SUBURBIA AGAIN

Perfect Front Lawns, version one

The perfect front lawn. It mattered in the 1980s—at least, in 1980s Australia, to my parents as first homeowners in a suburb where bees loved clover and I was always getting stung. Calamine lotion was my skin-upon-skin, a chalky holy water: ritual, penance, salve. It was my fault. Again, again, I tempted fate—trying to stand on my hands while my skirts became tents and my knickers frilly white-pink flags of uprise … and surrender.

I was defeated from the start for playing games good girls must outgrow. So I did. Grow. Outgrow. When and how? All I remember is one minute grass and bees, then the next a wall, a window and me inside, freckles paling, skirt ironed, sitting in place.

I remember watching my father with his Victa mower: up—back—up—back—his movements as straight, as uniform as the once-unruly turf was by Saturday afternoons, once he was done. I loved the mower's engine: vibrations through the floor. I loved going out to breathe in afterwards: cut blades and two-stroke. Sometimes when Dad pulled the start chain, the machine just coughed or did nothing at all. Unlike our next-door neighbour, he didn't shout, swear, or kick, but something about him would shrink, would crumble. These times made it even more magical when the chain worked, when the machine roared into life.

How would it feel—to start a mower with just one pull?

That question was not for me to answer. Good girls do not grow into such things.

I never mowed a lawn … Until, at thirty-five, I fell out of good and into the necessities of life for a woman never married yet legally divorced from a long-term partner. I got myself a second-hand mower. Unleaded, not two-stroke, but still with a pull chain—that roar, that thick petrol scent.

I struggled, at first, to start the thing. Some days I still do—especially when the grass grows too long. For the 1980s are gone. I'm neither a parent nor a first homeowner. I work and survive, like all of us do here, in the outer suburbs where land is cheap and other things too. The neighbours' lawns are overgrown like mine, some scattered with car parts. My mother doesn't visit. She screws her nose. But I can breathe here. The long grass feels safe. And then, some days, when the sun is out and the bees at work, it feels good to pull my mower from the shed, fill her with petrol, press the prime button—and then …

I get a feeling like standing on my hands inside a flapping tent of skirts.

Some days, it even starts with just one pull.

Through the Cracks, version ten

An ABC equation:
hot water
detergent
plates.

Feel justified
in this moment—and the next—and the next—

Flowers faded, replaced.

Standard issue
laminex and mortgages

—the farthest thing imaginable—

wine glasses
wine glasses
vegemite jars.

Right parts
in their rightful order.

Keep breathing.

Meanwhile, Back in Suburbia / Auto-cento ten

Again, again, I tempted fate
—trying to stand on my hands—I danced,

danced, danced, barely feeling the blisters,
legs racing like a panicked clockwork heart

Birth certificate. Driver's license.
No, no, no.

Make something—make sense—
sense beehives, their buzz.

Breath and heartbeat—words, bodies, touch—

Damn.
It was such a good party

—swimming—
—drowning—

Forgotten phone numbers
and poorly-wrapped wads of spent gum.

Too old for these games.

Try and be nice—unexpectedly simple.

Fix the clock.

Chronics, version one

Years ago, I shocked myself, trying to fix the oven clock. My error was daft, too daft to relay. The thing is, I was sad. Sadness makes me tired, and tiredness saddens me more. My tired, sad self thinks crooked, does thoughtless things. That day, I only knew I was fed up with the clock's four zeroes constantly flashing, making it always midnight. Those lightning blue Ohs gaped like square mouths, screaming where I was at:

Stuck—neither moving forward nor able to spin
back and reclaim all that had and was still
meanwhile racing past in lightning colours like warp
speed in some old-school lo-fi sci-fi, or one of
those amusement park rides that busts gravity
by spinning in place.

When I failed to fix the clock, I was thrown across the kitchen. I must have been, because I found myself on the floor. How long had I blacked out? The clock was still broken. Somebody was laughing. It was me. My body. My body was laughing. Hysterically. Why? It wasn't funny. Yet it was—funny-odd how straight away the sad-tiredness shifted. It was no longer midnight. I no longer even cared if the clock stayed broken. I, at least, was unstuck.

The next day, a school friend phoned from hospital. The doctors were saying she needed ECT. Could I get her out?

I went immediately.

White corridors. Everything retro space age. Not walking so much as being sucked along a breathless vortex. The ceiling veined by exposed pipes. No windows. Pine-o-clean mingling with salt damp.

When I found my friend, she said,

I used to be a lioness,
but those sharks, they've made me a goldfish.

I went to the nurses and asked, was there any other way?

Stop interfering. It's for the best.

When my friend got out, she said the same thing. The treatment had been necessary, had fixed her, she said.

A little while later, she was hospitalized again. Then back out. Then gone. Then back. Then. Then. Then.

The sad-tiredness I'd felt before my shock came back too. Then went. And came back. And went. Not for any obvious reason. Just with time, like breathing. Because my brain is my body is a clock: I breathe, I tick, I am rhythm, falling in and out. I still do daft things, frequently, but I stay well clear of anything wired. My oven clock remains broken, still flashing those lightning blue Ohs, like mouths.

Years later, it's sometimes still always midnight.

Sensing / Making, version ten

Houses. Then towers, halls, stations, malls, cemeteries.

A giant bed, waiting.

Busted limbs, hearts.
Mountains of quiet.

Time.

Loss.

Finally—

silence.

Taking Time, part two, version four

isolating
cold
collapsed
it stung

you said
you could die.

that last time—
your breath and heartbeat
words
bodies
touch

—never believed
with the others.

I wanted—Yes—

time.

Island, part two, version four

Damn.

Words bounced and echoed.
A rumbling ensued.
Shockwaves.
The tide.

Words still shaking.

Take it.
Let go.
Let go.

Let it fall from the sky—
fat, sharp splatters. For months,
shivering, wide awake, naked.

The storm raging until morning.
Then, sunshine—one ripe red globe

—ignored.

All morning, all afternoon.

Why?

For days and days

—nothing.

Continued growing, dying,
battling

—what islands do.

Collingwood Daze, version one

and then she was spinning towards me, pupils wide like the mouths of those sideshow clowns moving fast *toofast*, saying THIS is our San Fran our Paris our New York Set Match Bloomsbury and we're inside IT we are IT and one day we will look back on this night and and and and and and and and and and and and and and and and

we were at a party, one of those parties in one of those Collingwood houses where we hopscotched fits on the way to the mailbox—but hey, it kept the rent down, plus we hardly ever checked the mailbox—

and we were saying how it was such a good party the best party ever and we would never forget that party because everyone absolutely everyone was there at that party whichever party it was and so we were so proud that we were there

sprawled round some lounge room where the walls went at weird angles even when you weren't bent which we were, breathing whiskey like we were fish and it was water

we thought we were swimming. of course, we were drowning

and some of us even knew that, but it wasn't cool to mention, and we cared oh so much about cool, because we weren't, but had convinced one another we were because we were The Girls, each of us dating one of The Guys, those guys we believed were all undiscovered Kerouacs, not realising that Kerouac himself was for the most part an undiscovered Kerouac, and not much fun to be around

in the end Guy A and Guy B cheated on Girls B and C while my Guy locked me in the house and beat me round 'til I through-windowed it with Girl capital G who cheated on me with Boys XYYYYYYYYY

but none of this had happened then or ever would because we were in a loungeroom the loungeroom at a party the party and she was spinning, Girl C and or D or whoever she was, and she was saying THIS

is our San Fran our Paris our New York Set Match Bloomsbury and we're inside IT we are IT and one day we will and and and and and and and and

as her mouth kept moving spewing shapes and noises everything spinning around me made me suddenly carsick like a child, wondering, Where am I going? Why did it seem a good idea to climb aboard this thing? Is it too late to get off?

and that was the moment when our IT started being over. Like San Fran. Like Paris. Like New York Set Match Bloomsbury were all Over, long over and out

what's more, IT had never begun.

The Woman with the Disobedient Head, verison two

a peak-hour train carriage—anonymous knees
and elbows jutting, poking, jabbing

—only so many times the word 'sorry' can sound sincere
at this hour of the morning—

an empty beer bottle, the smell of glue, a kid
with earphones, gel in hair, hot chips and *doofdoofdoof*

<<*next stop city central*>>
<<*next stop city central*>>

train stops. shrill drone. doors part.
a breeze—momentary freedom—

Naming the Tortoise, part ten

'There is no tortoise', the child's father repeats, tone as immalleable as his folded-arm posture.

'But there is. It has a name. Its name is—'

'I don't want to know about the tortoise. I want you to put that away and go to bed. You're too old for these games.'

The child opens her mouth, then shuts it. She looks towards the tortoise, wishing it would say something. It stretches its neck, staring long and hard, but remains silent.

'There's no tortoise,' the child's father reiterates, his words forceful and heavy.

'There's no tortoise,' the child echoes softly.

THE BLACK SHOES, VERSION ONE

As a child I was told the story of a girl whose red shoes enslaved her, made her keep forever dancing.

Later, I would own a similar pair, except mine were black, purchased for work, worn with thick stockings and a pencil skirt in which I could take but the tiniest of steps, always in straight, straight lines. Yet that too is a kind of dancing, a moving to a beat, in this case one that beat me as I struggled to keep pace. Hence why I bought those shoes, as opposed to any other regulation black-with-closed-toe-and-small-hell-but-not-too-high-you've-got-to-walk-bitch pair on sale that day.

I wanted them for the sound they made, click clack, like castanets, announcing each footfall, reminding me and all around just how fast I was moving, to how regular a beat. Not a waltz, nor a tango, oh no, more like a march, a military two step in which I held my torso rigid, frenetic legs repeating patterns drilled a little deeper through each instant in which I followed and was led.

They made me able to keep up, those shoes, made the thought of falling out of line impossible, unthinkable. They made so much unthinkable and thus made me able to do other things, things I might otherwise have questioned. Their clicking, like a second hand, like the ticking of a bomb, reminded me there was no time for questions: *Bitch, you're paid to dance, so dance, dance to the song being played; don't suggest other rhythms; don't try to flip our disc.*

And so, in those shoes I danced, danced, danced, barely feeling the blisters, nor the aches in legs forever racing like a panicked clockwork heart. At night, though I kicked them off, I would find myself still dancing, taking orders in my sleep. Even now, years since wearing their soles to holes, years beyond the day I finally said I'd walk away, I catch myself sometimes saying No to some possibility I've not paused to consider. I catch myself falling in with certain rhythms, certain rituals, and if I ask myself why I can't say why. That's just how it is, how it seems it's always been. Then I look at my feet and see them still dancing, still so blistered. I hear the click clack like wagging tongues, like laughter, and I know, those damn shoes, they're still there.

Hungry, part ten

The woman stands, mouth open. There is nothing she can say.

The Official glances again at the clock.

'It's closing time. There is nothing I can do for you, I suggest you begin your journey home.'

The woman's thorax spasms and stretches with an uncomfortable quantity of air.

'Home ... ' she whispers.

The Official points towards the cliff face, then at a small basket just left of the box. The basket is labelled with black squiggles. If the woman could read them, she would know, they say, *Courtesy of The Department of New Beginnings*. But she doesn't need to read this to know what the basket contains: frayed rope. She glances at the cliff face, then back towards The Official. Her eyelids stretch so wide it seems the skin will split. Her body has forgotten how to blink.

ELEVEN: MORE BEAUTIFUL PEOPLE

Hungry, part eleven

The Official, tired from the day's work and eager to get home for dinner, gestures once more towards the cliff face before lowering a grille over the window. The Department of New Beginnings is shut now and will reopen in opening hours.

After a moment's pause, the woman begins banging on the window. She howls.

'My paper! My paper!'

Then, a string of undecipherable sounds.

The Official is already gone.

More Beautiful People / Auto-cento eleven

She never said a word about what happened.

There is nothing she can say.

still.
still.
Something is different now.

hazy shapes
float from place to place
in limbo

adrift

she dons a thick black scarf.

in quiet
still shaking
head down

its name hangs unspoken in every space

The clock reads three.

THE WOMAN WITH THE DISOBEDIENT HEAD, VERSION THREE

MaggieMem places a hand beneath her chin,
feigning nonchalance, revealing nothing
of the concentration it takes to keep her head in place.

why this morning, of all mornings?
she checklists events, trying to pin-point a cause.
perhaps the muffly *doofdoofdoof*—something to do with isotopes
and nano-scale mosh pits?

MaggieMem would never voice these notions, of course.

she used to try not thinking,
but the second she stopped thinking
about not thinking
the same old thoughts broke through
—even more numerous, more ridiculous—

these days MaggieMem just thinks and keeps her mouth shut.

she works in PR.
she is the front-desk receptionist.
she likes the smell of white-out in the mornings.

she might have achieved more
if not for her disobedient head.
whether she was born with it
or developed it
remains a topic of debate.

the severity fluctuates. sometimes, for months on end,
MaggieMem almost forgets to be frightened. then
absolutely nothing can hold in place.

sometimes the cause is obvious
other times, there is no explanation, no warning.

MaggieMem's head comes unstuck
because MaggieMem's head comes unstuck.

she has a stash of antibacterial wipes in her handbag.
she also has some dental floss, a sewing kit,
crumpled dockets, broken-lid lippies,
forgotten phone numbers,
and poorly-wrapped wads of spent gum.

at AlmostThirty she still can't decide
whether to like or hate attention.

after a mad dash through the city,
MaggieMem slides into the reception desk
—only one minute late—
smooths an imaginary crinkle in her shirt,
feigns indifference.

if she keeps her hair forward, nobody will notice.

she sighs.

Taking Time, part two, version five

cold
collapsed lung.

it stung
still.
still.

can't feel—
can't breathe—
can't sense—

breath?
heartbeat?

can't tell.

starved,
old,
metal,
strained.

something is different now.

take time.

Temping

A shadow on the move, she slips
through cracks in payrolls
and roster books, turning up
everywhere, belonging nowhere.

Lipstick stains
on someone's favourite coffee mug.
Paperwork
filed in illogical places.

Arriving with no future,
she leaves without a past
like a shunned lover tip toeing
from the bedroom before sunrise.
She'll be back when next needed.
And yes, eventually,
she's always needed,
whether wanted or not.

She has a name.
So do all the other hazy
shapes who float from place to place
like ghosts, in limbo, sheeted
in nondescript shirts
and standard-issue smiles,
playing whatever roles are cast
with bit-part actor gusto,

selling life
in eight-hour portions.

IMPOSSIBLE

She never said a word about what happened.

After she died, they scattered her ashes
at the end of an old paddock
and planted a tree:
a white gum
leaves grey-green
like her eyes.

It grew quickly at first,
a wooden explosion, sparks of leaves
shooting for the sky, sharp
and pointed as knives.

Over time, there was less green
and more grey, the trunk consumed
by lichen, black lichen
staining like mascara tear drops
while sap oozed, pooled
and congealed
like scabs

on branches growing gnarled
and knotted, impossible
to climb, impossible
to break.

Through the Cracks, version eleven

nice is an ABC equation:

flowers
boyfriend
unexpectedly
simple
warm
wonderful

fingers
patterns
liking
being the one
warm and safe
happy
breathing
home
wanted
kept
certain

Sensing / Making, version eleven

She wanted Sound. Taste. Touch.
Smell. Sight. Fright. Lust. Love. Motion. Emotion.
Fun. Humour. Occasion. Direction. South. East. Sky. Sea.
Waves, tides, and their rises. Moons and stars. Rhythms
and dancing—connection.

These, to her, all seemed like dreams.

She decided to make words into a world.
Fragile. Detailed. Like real.

She stood, trembling, opened an eye. Then
her tear ducts cried for the undressed ocean and waiting mouth.
She ground feathers and bones, made sculptures of beaches
inside mountains. She starved in quiet
and danced her everything left.

Her gifts turned away,
finally she stopped

and opened

silence.

Island, part two, version five

wild
flames
all but petered

breathed in,
breathed out.
still shaking

couldn't take it.
blew apart
screamed.

wild
wild.

washed away
kept raging
ripe red

That's what islands

Christmas Day in Kolkata

She grabbed my tit and said,
"I'll fuck you, mam".
Four feet tall, gap tooth grin
pasted over the snarl that echoed in her eyes,
her already shrivelled, ancient eyes.

I kept walking, head down,
lone white woman weaving through the slums
like a paper yacht around Cape Horn.

She may have been the minor,
but I was the one whose innocence cracked—
my body violated,
my understanding of all the world
undone.

Her unwelcome hand twisted
and gnawed me
long after I'd walked away.

Those words alone would have hurt as much.
What made her go and grab my tit?

She was the right age to be my daughter.

Naming the Tortoise, part eleven

The child's father takes the box. He puts it on a higher shelf this time, beyond the child's reach, chair or no chair.

'It's night. Go back to bed,' he tells her.

The child nods and makes her way to her room. The tortoise follows, its huge feet and gnarled yellow toenails padding with surprising delicacy across the kitchen linoleum, then the carpet.

The child waits until her father is out of earshot, then spins back to hiss,

'Shoo! You've caused enough trouble already.'

The tortoise sighs, but doesn't falter from its course, plodding on with its same rhythmic, nauseating pace. The child knows it is here for reasons that are not accidental. Though it may disappear in daylight, it will not leave, will not be gone. Not tonight, not tomorrow, not next year. Not until it has walked through every room in the house, opened every cupboard and touched every inch of floor. Not until its breath has entered every crack of every wall, until its name hangs unspoken in every space, every pause. And maybe still not then.

The clock reads three.

for Nobody, in Particular, part two

There was a girl whose tears were shapes
of Icarus. Their black wings blistered skin.
She swallowed bruises like they were bouquets,
wore scars for diamonds. She dressed

in woodsmoke and spoke in shades
of Autumn. Buried in her skin
were all the seasons, scarlet daffodils.
She kept her Springtime buried.

TWELVE: DÉJÀ VU

Déjà vu Again / Auto-cento thirteen

Last breath and heartbeat.

The water is rising.
Who remembers sand?

Such a stupid game—no control, spiralling
down, down, down.

Beer stains on the carpet—mouth shut—
a fee willingly paid.

White walls groaning, worrying.
Unglued. What a pain.

Hungry
Hungry.
Hungry.

—unfortunate, but irrelevant.

Wanted to know
connection.

sobbed
sobbed

S.O.S.

—a dark shape, ever larger.

Taking Time, part two, version six

still, still. still—that last

breath and heartbeat
—words
—bodies
—animals—

believed
in—

now—shattered—

wanted
time.

Waking Up to White, version two

A colour.
Not a colour.
A not-colour.

Absence.

Go. Don't go.
Surrender.

Australia is Forty Six Celsius. Trash
washing down storm pipes. Out, out.
The water is rising. Houses swallowed.
Who remembers sand?
Snow?
Bread?

Careful.

Blood stains.
Ambulance.
Big bag and plastic zipper.
Barely creased sheets, stripped away.

The smell of detergent.
The smell of white.

Snakes and Ladders, version two

Such a stupid game. No control, beyond cheating.

Otherwise, everything left to gravity
and landing right.

Sometimes, so close …

Then,

spiralling down down down

into consequences,
shame—guilty—condemned.

In truth,

it taught a lot about life.

Stupid game.

Through the Cracks, version twelve

dishes
dishes

filthy, out of order
make them clean—new again—

at two, three, four a.m.

hot water,
chilblains

plates of seventies vintage—big flowers
once lime green, orange, brown—

beer stains on the carpet

a simple solution to this moment—and the next—and the next—

mouth shut,
glassware before crockery

THE GAME OF BARBIES, VERSION TWO

Played—and played and played and played and played

the game of Barbies—Because

good at it, knew how to win.

Yes, there is winning with Barbies.

Points are tallied and prizes awarded,
fouls called, offenders disqualified.

Boundaries and goalposts shift. But that's the point.

What makes winning at Barbies so special
and so hard is that getting good is not the same as winning

—a fee willingly paid.

Déjà vu / Auto-cento twelve

White walls groaning, worrying.
A field of scarlet daffodils.
She ate an apple and slept for a long time.
Make, make, make sense—*please*.

Electronic music repeats itself
—*yeah yeah ooh baby*
ooh yeah baby doll—
Common and uncommon dreams
recurring differently—Falling

from the top floor, never hitting the ground.
Bruises. Planets. Marbles. Blood.
Unfolding purely to die
and so become alive again.

It was such a good party
—swimming—
—drowning—
Something is different now.
The clock reads three.

THE WOMAN WITH THE DISOBEDIENT HEAD, VERSION FOUR

unglued. in a peak-hour train carriage. what a pain.
a sharp aroma. bodies of strangers. anonymous knees
and elbows jutting, poking, jiggling and jabbing.
a balancing act: keep head in place.

why this morning, of all mornings?

a hot rivulet darts. damn.

electronic music repeats itself.
yeah yeah ooh baby ooh yeah baby doll.

isotopes jiggling and clashing.
try not thinking. mouth shut.

<<*next stop city central*>>
<<*next stop city central*>>

the train stops. doors part.

running through a crowded train station with no head.

silent curses (waiting in line).
a cubicle. *thud* (the door).
cler-ick (the lock).
sigh.

one-by-two metres of solitude. bliss!
not worrying what anybody thinks.
naked breeze, freedom from the head.
how lovely it would be.

Hungry, version two

a plateau, cliff face, desert, volcanoes—a box—

square white placard, black squiggles:
age, race, gender, style of dress, psycho-spiritual persuasion,
and ice-cream flavour preferences …

Hungry
Hungry.
Hungry.

unfortunate, but irrelevant to the application

Hungry.

sounds, language—problem: mouth—
ocean waves, grooves and hollows, songs
there is no point singing here

Hungry.
Hungry.

a state, not a name

Hungry—true.

a silkworm, surrounded by noisy schoolchildren,
a sealed-up box, a cling-wrap window, a few pinprick holes

Not Stupid. Hungry.
Hungry. Nothing but Hungry.

want to change, be New. New Begin.

papers, a notebook, precious,
stained, crinkled,
smudged inky scribblings,
dates
—more than one hand has added to this book—
thick and old, less than half-way full

Identity.
surrendered.

Birth certificate. Driver's license. A bank letter or a phone bill …

No, no, no.
It's closing time.
Begin your journey home.'

Sensing / Making, version twelve

The mouth
wanted
To know
connection

decided
to make
words
the world.

The eye
stewed
then cried
for the ocean.

looked
inside mountains
in quiet
and closed

until finally

Island, part two, version six

ignored

wouldn't stop
sobbed
sobbed

days and days
longed for soft

remained huddled
rolled over

S.O.S.

flung out
pulled in.
disappeared.

Naming the tortoise, part twelve

Back in bed now, bladder emptied, belly soft, the child still stirs. Still, sleep seems so far away. Or perhaps she's been asleep and dreaming this whole time—dreaming that she can't sleep.

That must be it. She's been dreaming, and is still. For there, in her room's corner, is the tortoise. And, echoing ever louder in her head, the memory of a sound she's never heard and cannot make, but lives with and carries all the same.

Yes, the tortoise has a name. The child knows it now, just as she knows she must never speak this name aloud, not even just to herself. The sheets are even colder than before. The tortoise remains in the corner, a dark shape, ever larger.

Alogopoiesis
by Amelia Walker

This book was written on Kaurna Yerta, the lands of the Kaurna people. I pay respect to Kaurna Elders, past and present, and to all First Nations people.

Acknowledgement for poems previously published is made to the following anthologies and journals: 'Naming the tortoise' *Naming the Tortoise and Other Stories: Gawler Short Story Competition Anthology*; 'Through the cracks, version one' *Meniscus*; 'Through the cracks, version two' *Abridged*; 'Woman buying fish' and 'Owned' *Blue Dog*; 'Sensing/Making, version one' and 'Chronics', ScAN: Science Arts Network; 'Taking time', parts one and two, *The Incompleteness Book*; 'The woman with the disobedient head', *Voiceworks*; 'Island' and 'Impossible', *Poetrix*; 'Marked', *Not Very Quiet*; 'How to Get Inside an Orange', 'Red Shoes', 'Marilyn on the Electric Chair', 'The pornography in clouds' and 'The science of breathing out' *Feast Festival Anthology*; 'Waking up to white' and 'Gone Up' (Intermission) *Unusual Work*; 'A Story (not) about Green' *Golfo*; 'Blue, version one' *The Haight-Ashbury Literary Review*; 'Blue, version two' *Algebra of Owls*; 'Language Lesson', 'Small Questions too Daft to Ask' and 'Hatshepsut' *Page Seventeen*; 'Sundori' *Social Alternatives*; 'For Nobody, in particular', *Blue Giraffe*; 'The game of Barbies' and 'Snakes and Ladders', in *Reimagining the Academy: ShiFting Towards Kindness, Connection, and an Ethics of Care*; 'The Black Shoes' *Dancing the Light*; 'Women like that' *The Journal of Gender-Based Violence*; 'Small Questions too large to ask'; 'The day they took the plants away' *Poetry and Sustainability in Education*; 'Kite' Taslima Nasrin's Blog.

First published 2023

POETRY

ISBN: 978-0-6456337-8-8

BOOK, TYPSETTING, AND LOGO DESIGN
Mountains Brown Press

PUBLISHER
Life Before Man

Gazebo Books
PO Box 375
Summer Hill
New South Wales 2130
Australia

gazebobooks.com.au/life-before-man/

2 4 6 8 10 9 7 5 3 1

This book was made possible thanks to Anthony Mark Day

COVER IMAGE: *Bundle*, 2023, oil on linen, 26 x 20.5 cm, © Phil Day

ISBN 978-0-6456337-8-8